ALDERBURY
WAR MEMORIALS

In Freedom's Cause

THE ALDERBURY & WHADDON
LOCAL HISTORY RESEARCH GROUP

ALDERBURY WAR MEMORIALS

In Freedom's Cause

by

MARY HINCHCLIFF & BERNICE RANGE

foreword by

**MAJOR GENERAL ANTONY
MAKEPEACE-WARNE**

Published by

THE ALDERBURY & WHADDON
LOCAL HISTORY RESEARCH GROUP
2004

First published by
Alderbury & Whaddon Local History Research Group,
Hawthorns, Old Road, Alderbury, Salisbury, Wiltshire, United Kingdom

ISBN 0-9538004-1-5

ALDERBURY & WHADDON LOCAL HISTORY RESEARCH GROUP

The Alderbury & Whaddon Local History Research Group was formed in 1998 by some enthusiastic amateur local historians determined to write a village history for the Millennium. The Group has continued with its research projects into the history of the parish, its buildings, institutions and people. It meets monthly for discussion and welcomes new members with a research interest. The Group has a website www.alderbury.org.uk and has started an archive to collect items of information, family genealogy, documents, letters, photographs or anything connected with the parish. If anyone owns or knows of anything that might be of interest to the Group please contact any of the members.

MEMBERS 2004

Margaret Smale (Chair)
Mary Hinchcliff (Secretary)
Brian Johnson (Treasurer)
Veronica Dodkins
Peter M Hammond
Christine Marr
Bernice Range
Ian Strong

Also by the same Group
Alderbury & Whaddon: A Millennium Mosaic of People, Places and Progress

ACKNOWLEDGEMENTS

Maps **CHRISTINE MARR**   *Additional research* **PETER M HAMMOND**
llustrations **JUNE BRIND**   *Indexing* **BRIAN JOHNSON**
Design **FRANCES MARR**   *Printing* **SALISBURY PRINTING CO LTD**

We would like to thank all those who have contributed in any way to the making of this book especially the editorial committee for their hard work in making it presentable. We are also grateful to the Commonwealth War Graves Commission for permission to use the information on its website. Finally, we thank our husbands, David Hinchcliff and Bill Range, who have been so understanding and supportive.

We are indebted to the many relatives and friends of the fallen for their help and support and to the various Ministry of Defence (MOD) departments, regimental museums and record offices who opened their archives for this research.

Edward Albery
E.A. Angel
Brigadier Frank Bevan
Mrs U. Blackman
Bob Burns
Mrs J Cannings
AVM Christie-Miller
Mrs Ann Clarke
Ivor Cross
Mrs Jacqueline Dart
Mrs Margery Dobbs
Leslie Foyle
Mrs Audrey Grant
John Hatcher

Trevor Hayward
Terry Hissey
Captain Horne
Tony Howe
Mick Kelly
Christopher Kirkby
Tina Kirkby
Daryl Knight
Paula Knight
Peggy Ling
Tony Morrel
Bob Newman
Ken Nicholson
Mrs Norris

Christopher Norris
Mrs Beryl Parry
Colonel Porral
Sally Roberts
Clive Rolls
Colonel Taylor
Mrs Patricia Tozer
Peter Tucker
Robert Underhill
Bob Verner-Jeffries
Mrs Verner-Jeffries
Miss Louisa Wathen
Frank Woodrow

Organisations and individuals

The National Archives of Australia, Canberra
The National Archives of Canada, Ottawa
Jim Parker, The Machine Gun Corps voluntary archivist
Terry Hissey, The George Cross Database
Roberta Hazan, archivist, St Dunstan's, charity for blind ex-service personnel
Ministry of Defence, Directorate of Personal Services (Army)
David Chilton, Curator. The Royal Gloucestershire, Berkshire & Wiltshire Regiment (Salisbury) Museum
Captain Horne, Curator, Guards Museum, Birdcage Walk, London
West Sussex Records Office
Dept of Research and Information Services, Royal Air Force Museum, Hendon
Tony Banham, a Hong Kong based researcher

CONTENTS

FOREWORD 9

MAPS, ILLUSTRATIONS & PHOTOGRAPHS 10

PREFACE 11

WORLD WAR I 13

INTRODUCTION 14

CHAPTER 1   WAR ON LAND AND SEA 15
Sydney Hazel

CHAPTER 2   THE WESTERN FRONT 1916 20
Ernest Bundy, Thomas Pearman, Edward Hatcher,
Arthur Bundy, Thomas Bundy, John Hatcher

CHAPTER 3   THE GALLIPOLI CAMPAIGN 1915 - 16 31
Edgar Mouland

CHAPTER 4   THE MIDDLE EAST 35
Alfred Howe, Harry Prewett, Hugh Tozer, Hedley Rolls,
Charles Albery, Ernest Hatcher

CHAPTER 5   THE WESTERN FRONT 1917 44
William Ingram, Wilfred Mouland,
Walter Bundy, Francis Harper

CHAPTER 6   GREECE & ITALY 1915 – 18 53
Charles Beaven, Albert Northeast

CHAPTER 7   THE WESTERN FRONT 1918 56
Frederick Hatcher, Henry John Sims, Archibald Burt, Reynold Rolls
Robert Bundy, Maurice Kerly, Leslie Northeast

CHAPTER 8   WAR CASUALTIES SENT HOME 68
Harry Musselwhite, Edward Earney

SURVIVORS OF THE GREAT WAR NAMED ON ST MARY'S PLAQUE 71

GALLANTRY AWARDS WWI 72

NOTES 74

WORLD WAR II

INTRODUCTION   78

CHAPTER 9   WESTERN EUROPE 1939 – 40   79
F.W. Carter

CHAPTER 10   FAR EAST 1941   83
N. Wathen, E.G. Grout

CHAPTER 11   TUNISIA 1942 – 3   90
A.W.T. Hatcher

CHAPTER 12   ITALY 1943 – 4   94
R.C. McLeod

CHAPTER 13   THE ROYAL AIR FORCE 1942 – 3   98
J.W.C. Kidd, J.W. Snook

CHAPTER 14   WESTERN EUROPE 1944 – 5   103
M.V. Christie-Miller, J. Woodrow, W.C. Witt

CHAPTER 15   THE ROYAL NAVY   110
S. Gumbleton

CHAPTER 16   WAR CASUALTIES WHO DIED IN THE UK   114
S. Mitchell, S.A.H. Kirkby, W. Foster, C. Turner, C.E. Bearman

CHAPTER 17   POST WAR   120

SOURCES   122

BIBLIOGRAPHY   126

INDEX   127

FOREWORD

It is appropriate that this well researched and moving account is in the nature of a companion volume to 'Alderbury & Whaddon: A Millennium Mosaic of People, Places and Progress'. We should all reflect from time to time that a price had to be paid that we might continue to enjoy such 'people, places and progress'.

Very few of the men who feature in this book were professional soldiers, sailors or airmen. However, whether volunteer or conscript all recognized that their way of life was under threat and that things would not be normal again until the enemy had been defeated. Hostilities were to cause an interruption to family, career and social life and many personal aspirations had to be temporarily put on one side. For most of those in this book that interruption was to be permanent.

One can only be profoundly moved by the lives described so well in this book and the manner of their ending. Some died in the heat of battle, some in the appalling conditions of a Japanese prisoner of war camp, and some in what we would now call 'friendly fire' incidents. Gratitude for their sacrifice is tinged with sadness and wonder at the indiscriminate nature of death and injury in war. The best way we can honour the debt we owe is perhaps to seek to uphold and protect the values for which they died.

I commend this book to readers of all ages. It is the story of ordinary people caught up in extraordinary events – we will remember them.

Antony Makepeace-Warne
Major General

Salisbury June 2004

MAPS, ILLUSTRATIONS & PHOTOGRAPHS

WWI

Drawing – Copy of Lord Kitchener poster

Map – Western Front showing German Advance, August 1914

Map – Scapa Flow and Marwick Head

Map – Location of Canadian 1st CMR at Battle of Mount Sorrel, Ypres

Map – Somme Region, 1 July – 18 Nov 1916

Map – Mash Valley

Map – Ginchy

Map – Pozières, Mouquet Farm, and Thiepval,

Map – Mametz, the Bazentins and High Wood

Map – St Pierre Vaast Wood

Map – Constantinople, Dardanelles and Gallipoli

Map – Gallipoli Peninsula

Map – Mesopotamia

Map – Palestine

Map – River Ancre valley

Map – Vimy Ridge

Map – Area between rivers Souchez and Scarpe

Map – Western Front, July 1917

Map – Salonika

Map – Northern Italy

Map – Flesquières, Welsh Ridge

Map – German Spring Offensive 1918

Map – Pacault Wood

Photocopy of the postcard sent by Maurice Kerly to his parents

Map – Damery and Parvillers: Battle of Amiens

WWII

Map – Battle of Flanders

Map – Hong Kong

Map – Singapore

Map – Burma-Siam Railway

Map – Tunisian Theatre

Map – Tripoli to Salerno route

Map – Salerno Bridgehead, Battipaglia area

Map – Invasion plan

Map – Landing beaches and bridgehead

Map – The Breakout and main advances

WWI PHOTOGRAPHS

Headstone of Edward Hatcher's grave

Charles Ernest Albery

Photograph of a postcard sent from India by Charles Albery to his family in England

Hugh Tozer

Ernest Hatcher

Alderbury Village Band c1914

Thiepval Memorial

Charles Hazel Beaven

Maurice Kerly

Harry Musselwhite

WWII PHOTOGRAPHS

Dunkirk Memorial

Dunkirk Memorial Window

Walter Norman Wathen

Edward George Grout

Roderick McLeod

John Walter Cameron Kidd

Jack Snook

Michael Vandeleur Christie-Miller

Jack Woodrow

Stanley Gumbleton

Samuel Alexander Holwell Kirkby

William Foster

Charles Turner

Celebration party for returning forces personnel, 1947

PREFACE

The Alderbury War Memorial stands on The Green, a pleasant part of old Alderbury. Erected about 1922, it comprises a column of Chilmark stone with a stepped plinth surmounted by a cross within a circle. Inscribed on the column are the names of the servicemen of Alderbury, Whaddon and Clarendon, who fell in the two World Wars.

There are further memorials inside the Alderbury Parish Church of St Mary. A stone wall-plaque, mounted after the Great War, lists the names and regiments of those who died and, unusually, of those who served and survived. An oak screen carved in classical style records the names and regiments of those who fell in World War II. There is a small inlaid tablet dedicated to a member of the Home Guard who won the George Cross in 1942. The church cemetery contains graves and headstones of soldiers who for various reasons are not identified on the other memorials.

Every year, during the Church Remembrance Service in November, the names of 38 men who died in the wars are solemnly read out. Who were they? Where did they serve? What happened to them? In this book we have endeavoured to answer these questions, or at least to shed some light on the circumstances in which they died.

The book is divided into two sections followed by appendices and a bibliography. The first section is concerned with World War I and the second with World War II. Each has been independently researched and written. Throughout, the term 'Alderbury men' is used loosely to denote anyone commemorated in or connected to, the parish, whether or not they were born or brought up in the locality. We claim no special knowledge of military matters and any errors are entirely ours. However, we have investigated extensively the campaigns in which these men fought, basing our research on a close study of documents, unit war diaries, regimental histories, family information, censuses, maps, contemporary newspapers and, where available individual service records. Commentary on the wider aspects of the two wars serves to put the circumstances involving local men into context. Sources used are listed with explanatory notes in the appendices. We have tried to be as accurate as possible in the face of much that will forever remain unknown.

Alderbury men served, and died, in diverse places: on the Western Front; in the mountains of northern Italy; across the deserts of the Middle East; amid the scrub-covered hills of Gallipoli; along the notorious Burma Railway; at Dunkirk; on the high seas and in the skies. Some were captured and interned in prisoner of war camps: three ended their days there.

Researching and writing this book has helped us to remember with gratitude, that the freedom we now take for granted is because of these men and those like them. This book is our tribute to them.

SECTION ONE

WORLD WAR I

....Short days ago
We lived, felt dawn,
saw sunset glow
Loved and were loved....

from 'In Flanders Field'
by John McRae
(1872-1918)

by

MARY HINCHCLIFF

INTRODUCTION

By the end of the First World War (WWI) or the Great War as it became known, nearly nine million people had been mobilised in the British Forces and three-quarters of a million had died. An estimated 136 men enlisted from Alderbury, Whaddon and Clarendon and 28 of these lost their lives. Most of them were volunteers.

Before conscription early in 1916, a volunteer could usually enlist in a regiment of his own choosing. A conscript was assigned to a unit by the army. For the new recruit several months of hard training followed. Then he would embark for a transit camp in France or another theatre of war. He would be attached to a platoon in one of the battalion's four companies, given his cap badge and transported up to the line.

At the front his company would spend a few days in a fire trench facing the enemy across the barbed-wire strewn desolation of no-man's-land. The constant cacophony of artillery fire and exploding shells was a shocking experience to many new soldiers. Here, perhaps, in the foetid dampness of a rat-ridden trench, or in the heat and dust of a fly-infested desert, a young volunteer might well have regretted his initial eagerness to enlist. By day he and his companions would be on the alert over the sandbagged parapet: night-time might find him on patrol, venturing across the barricade on his hands and knees into enemy territory. There would be times when he waited tensely for the signal that would send them all 'over the top'. In the ferocity of battle he would witness grim scenes of carnage, of friend and foe alike. The probability of being killed, wounded, captured, gassed, or the victim of disease, was an everyday reality.

Out of the line, he would eat a proper meal, catch up on some sleep, bathe, and rid himself of the irritating fleas and lice that infested his body. He would be assigned to building trenches, digging graves, sandbagging, repairing wire, carrying supplies, weapon training and route marching. A strict code of discipline and smartness was always maintained with frequent parades and inspections. Competitive sports and football or rugby matches were arranged for recreation. A division might be sent to recuperate at some safer haven, to practise for a forthcoming attack or given leave to visit a nearby town for a few carefree hours. All too soon he would be going back to the front again.

In this section I have endeavoured to follow the military careers of these Alderbury men during the Great War, that most destructive and horrific of conflicts, to discover the circumstances that cost them their lives. They typify the experiences of millions of others from the British Commonwealth, and tens of millions across the globe.

CHAPTER 1

WAR ON LAND AND SEA

STORM CLOUDS GATHER

The Great War began in Europe but soon spread to other continents as colonies, dominions and countries with interests at stake, were drawn into the conflict. On one side were the Central Powers consisting principally of Germany, Austria-Hungary and from 1915, Turkey and Bulgaria. Allied against them were France, Britain, Belgium, Russia, Italy and later, many other countries. America, neutral at first, joined with the Allies in 1917.

By the start of the 20th century a new unified Germany had become the predominant growth area of Europe, both militarily and economically. The Kaiser and his elitist officer-class had expansionist ambitions, seeking world power. Germany's great industrial strength endeavoured to build a navy strong enough to challenge that of Britain and to arm a large conscripted army. By 1914, the country was well prepared to contest a war.

Germany's main ally, the dual monarchy of Austria and Hungary, sought to control her discontented Slav minorities and her independent neighbour, Serbia. France, embittered over the annexation of Alsace and Lorraine after the Franco-Prussian war of 1870, distrusted Germany's expansionist ambitions and forged a Triple Entente with Russia and Britain. In Russia, the Tsar ruled over a largely feudal nation of some 164 million people. For her own territorial ambitions, Russia championed the cause of the discontented Slavs of south-eastern Europe but military defeats and social unrest brought Russia close to revolution in the early years of the century. This came to a head in 1917 as the Bolsheviks took control of the country, murdering the Tsar and his family.

Britain was a very wealthy country, heavily industrialised, technically advanced and possessing the greatest naval force ever known. She also had the largest empire. However, the British standing army, though highly professional, was small in comparison with other Great Powers of Europe. Since the end of the Second Boer War, the army had been mainly deployed policing India, South Africa and Egypt.

In June 1914, the assassination of the heir-apparent to the Austro-Hungarian throne during his State visit to Sarajevo, sparked a chain of events that led to the outbreak of the Great War. Austria accused Serbia of complicity in the crime and sent an unacceptable ultimatum. Russia mobilised to protect Serbia and then Austria declared war on Serbia. The balance of power across Europe was broken. On the first day of August 1914, Germany declared war on Russia and then, as French mobilisation began, on France. Germany was at war on both Eastern and Western fronts.

THE STORM UNLEASHED

Almost immediately German armies swept into neutral Belgium in order to overwhelm and disable France from the north before Russia could fully mobilise. As a guarantor of Belgium's neutrality, Britain demanded Germany's withdrawal. When this ultimatum went unanswered, Britain proclaimed war against Germany on 4 August 1914. Six infantry divisions of the regular army, plus a cavalry division, raced across the English Channel to meet the Germans at Mons in Belgium. The Kaiser reportedly derided this 'contemptibly small' army, thus coining the use of 'Old Contemptibles' as the regulars' self-styled nickname. Reservist and Territorial units were mobilised and the dominions of Australia, New Zealand, Canada and South Africa sent battalions to swell Britain's force. Lord Kitchener, Minister for War, spearheaded a recruitment campaign

calling for 100,000 men aged between 18 and 30 to form a new volunteer force, or 'Kitchener's Army', as it became known. His target was met within a fortnight, reached half a million by mid-September and a million by November. It was not until the beginning of 1916, due to mounting casualties, that conscription had to be enforced and the upper age limit increased. For the present, volunteers came from every level of society and occupation, with some towns forming 'Pals' battalions in order to fight together. The expectation was that the war would be over by Christmas.

Despite a courageous stand, Germany's superior numbers and firepower forced the British Expeditionary Force (BEF) to fight a rear-guard action at Mons. Then, with heavy casualties, it withdrew southwards to regroup. The German armies swept through north-eastern France towards Paris in their bid for a quick, outright victory. This did not happen. Together, the British and French forces countered and halted their progress only 30 miles from the capital with successes on the River Marne and across the River Aisne. Then, in a series of flanking movements, the two sides began the 'race to the sea'. The Belgian army could not prevent Antwerp from falling and struggled to contain the Germans from occupying the whole of Belgium. In desperation the sluice gates along the Yser Canal were opened, flooding the area with seawater at high tide and halting further German advance. In late October, at the First Battle of Ypres,

British and Indian troops barred the way to the Channel ports of Calais and Boulogne, defending a salient that projected into occupied territory around the town of Ypres. The German army could not break through and heavy November snow brought an end to mobile warfare. For the next three years the war on the Western Front became one of stalemate, fought from behind lines of trench networks that stretched from the North Sea coast to the Swiss border. With ever more powerful and deadly armaments, the size of the casualty lists became unparalleled in history. On the Western Front alone, within the first six months of the war, the combatants suffered around two million men killed or wounded.

Western Front showing German Armies Advance August 1914

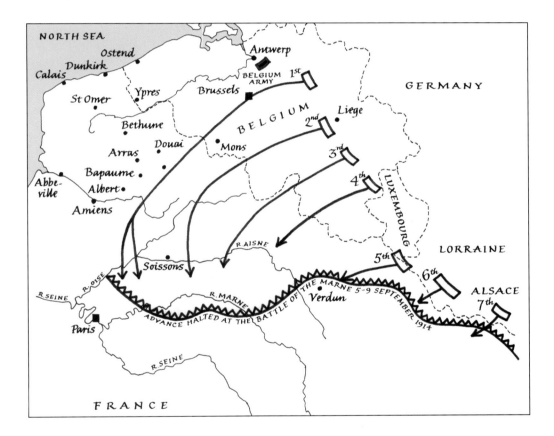

THE WAR AT SEA: 1914-16

The Royal Navy, Britain's senior service, was the key element in Britain's defence. At the outbreak of war Britain had the numerical advantage of dreadnoughts and battlecruisers and the British Empire allowed British ships access to ports across the world's oceans. The fleet patrolled the North Sea and the English Channel, searching and preventing ships from entering or leaving the ports of the Central Powers – a policy of starvation and isolation. Germany retaliated by blockading English coastal waters, laying mines and using submarine warfare to destroy shipping: the liner *Lusitania* with many Americans aboard was one of the victims, sunk off the Irish coast in 1915. This strategy was highly successful considering the huge number of ships destroyed but eventually it became one of the factors that brought America to the Allied side in 1917.

The two Grand Fleets met only once, at the Battle of Jutland on 31 May 1916. Ships were sunk on both sides, in fact more British than German, but the German Fleet did not risk operating in the North Sea again. Increasingly Germany turned to indiscriminate use of U-boats that could roam the oceans, lay mines and strike anywhere at will. It was just such a mine, laid by a German submarine that cost the life of Alderbury's young sailor, Sydney Hazel, aboard *HMS Hampshire*, on 5 June 1916.

SYDNEY HAZEL

J/31460 Ordinary Seaman
HMS Hampshire, Royal Navy
Died 5 June 1916. Aged 18

Sydney Hazel was born in Romsey in 1898, son of William and Alice Ann Hazel who lived in Ferry Cottage at Shute End, Alderbury. From here the Hazel family had operated the ferry crossing over the River Avon to Britford for more than a century. Sydney had a sister Gwen and a brother Tom, a Petty Officer on *HMS Venus*. Sydney joined the Royal Navy for a 12-year period in June 1914, at 16 years of age, only weeks before the war started. In his application he described his employment as 'garden boy'. For the next eight months he learned seamanship skills on the *Impregnable*, a static training ship for boys at Devonport, and then, from February to October 1915, aboard the *Agincourt*. He was then based in Portsmouth at the Royal Naval Establishment, *HMS Victory*, before being assigned to the battle cruiser *Hampshire* on 8 March 1916, with the rank of ordinary seaman. It is likely that he would have been aboard the *Hampshire* at the Battle of Jutland where the ship was in the second line of support but never actually engaged in the battle. This took place only six days before the Hampshire's tragic, final demise elsewhere.

Memorial Plaque awarded to Sydney Hazel

On 5 June 1916, the *Hampshire* set out from the naval base at Scapa Flow escorted by two destroyers. She was on an important, secret mission. The ship was carrying Field Marshal Earl Kitchener, the Secretary for War and Britain's most famous national hero. He and his staff were bound for Archangel in Russia where they were to meet the Tsar for a Council of War. The ships sailed into a force-nine gale and at the last minute the route had been changed, supposedly to a more sheltered westerly one. Unfortunately, this route had not been recently swept for mines, possibly due to the terrible weather. The sea was very rough and the two escorts fell behind and were ordered back to base. The *Hampshire* continued on alone. At 7.40pm, about a mile and a half off the cliffs of Marwick Head on the west coast of Orkney, an explosion shook the ship and as smoke bellowed out from a hole in her keel, she

Scapa Flow and Marwick Head where the Hampshire went down

began to sink rapidly. It was said that Lord Kitchener was observed in his greatcoat standing calmly on the forebridge. He was never seen again. Only 12 of the crew survived managing to get ashore clinging to life rafts, more dead than alive. Sydney Hazel was one of the 643 men lost. The ship had hit a mine laid a few days earlier by the German U-boat 75. Inevitably, because of the secrecy of the mission and the confusion after the sinking, there has been speculation and conspiracy theories in the press – that the ship was carrying gold to Russia, that Kitchener's death was pre-planned, that rescue attempts were deliberately prevented.

The wreck is now an official war grave and lies upside down on the seabed about 65 metres below the surface.[1] Sydney Hazel is commemorated at the Portsmouth Naval Memorial, Hampshire. There is also a monument and a Book of Remembrance at Winchester Cathedral. He was awarded the British War Medal and the Victory Medal.

CHAPTER 2

THE WESTERN FRONT 1916

BELGIUM: JUNE 1916, YPRES

At the beginning of June 1916, an Alderbury man serving with the 1st Canadian Mounted Rifles, by that time converted to infantry, was killed defending the Ypres Salient. He was Pte Ernest Bundy. It can be seen from the church memorial plaque that ten Alderbury men joined Canadian battalions, four of whom were killed in action. The attestation papers of those four soldiers reveal that they enlisted in Canada and were brought back to Britain for extra training before serving on the Western Front. There is no clue as to the reason they had gone to Canada, or for how long they had resided there before enlisting. It is interesting that of the first 34,000 volunteers to enlist in Canada, 65% of the rank and file and 29% of the officers were born in the British Isles or elsewhere in the Empire.[2] The four Canadian Divisions went on to win a reputation as intrepid and determined fighters and it is noteworthy that ten Alderbury men were among them. Of the 418,000 men who served overseas in the Canadian army, over 56,500 died.

ERNEST NOYCE BUNDY
114142 Private
1st Canadian Mounted Rifles (Saskatchewan Regiment)
8th Brigade 3rd Canadian Division,
Died 5 June 1916. Aged 20

Ernest was the youngest son of Evelyn and Edward Bundy of 37 Silver Street, Alderbury. All their three sons, William, Ernest, and Arthur enlisted with the Canadians, but only William survived. They had four sisters, Laura, Cecily, Lavinia and Winifred. Ernest Bundy joined up with the 9th Battalion at Sewell Camp, Manitoba, on 19 August 1915 age 19 years and seven months. On his enlistment papers he described himself as a farmer, unmarried, 5ft 5ins tall with dark-brown hair and blue eyes. His unit sailed from Canada to England in late autumn, arriving at Bramshot on 3 December 1915. It was sent to France in January 1916 as the 1st Canadian Mounted Rifles (CMR) of the 3rd Canadian Division.

    The newly formed 3rd Canadian Division was immediately posted to the waterlogged trenches of Flanders in chilly wintry weather where their comrades, the 1st and 2nd Canadian Divisions, were defending a six-mile front to the south of the Ypres Salient. It was here, less than a year earlier, that the Canadians had braved the first horrifying attacks of poisonous gas. The salient, a network of trenches on land projecting into enemy territory, was the most dangerous part of the Allied line and with the enemy surrounding three sides, it became the most fought-over battle-ground of the war. Even a small amount of lost ground could be strategically disastrous for the Allies. The 3rd Division's arrival provided welcome relief for the Canadian Corps who had been engaged in harassing enemy trenches with sniping and surprise artillery raids.

When Pte Ernest Bundy first arrived in France he was beset with foot problems and spent time in rest stations at Calais and in the field. He was diagnosed with ptomaine poisoning (a result of putrefaction caused by bacterial poisoning) and between 17 and 24 May he went into the hospital in Le Havre for seven days. He rejoined his unit at the Ypres Salient a few days before the start of the Battle of Mount Sorrel.

The four battalions of the Canadian 3rd Division were in a forward position on the most easterly projection of the Salient, the only part that had never been in enemy hands. The Canadians held a view over enemy trenches from the small hillock of Mount Sorrel and two higher ones known as Hill 61 and Hill 62 (or Tor Top). For six weeks the Germans had been covertly practising a plan to capture these positions. The 8th Brigade,

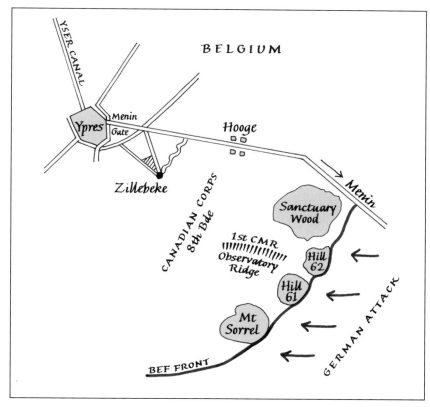

Location of 1st CMR. Battle of Mount Sorrel, Ypres 2 June 1916

which included Ernest Bundy's battalion, was deployed defending Observatory Ridge, a broad spur of farmland – and one of the enemy's objectives!

Early on the morning of 2 June, a bombardment burst above the Canadian lines and for the next four hours pounded their positions. The battles intensified along Observatory Ridge and Mount Sorrel and heavy casualties were incurred during the day. Surprisingly, in the evening, batteries of enemy machine guns failed to follow up their advantage but even so, 600 – 700 yards of valuable ground was in German hands. Counter-attacks by the Canadians over the following days could not regain all the lost ground, although much of the old line was recovered later in June. [3]

Pte Ernest Bundy was reported missing between 2 – 5 June and officially he was presumed to have died on 5 June 1916. He is commemorated at Railway Dugouts Burial Ground, 11.B.12, Zillebeke, Ypres (now Ieper) West Vlaanderen, Belgium. He was awarded the British War Medal and the Victory Medal.

FRANCE: THE SOMME, JULY 1916

Until the summer of 1916, the Somme was a relatively quiet and scenic region of the Western Front. However, the area was chosen to stage a large Anglo-French offensive across a 25-mile front. The objectives were threefold: to advance deeply into occupied territory; to relieve pressure on the French in the battle at Verdun that had been raging since the early spring; and to divert German manpower and arms from other theatres of war. For the first time the British Command under Field Marshall Haig, was able to plan the strategy of a major battle using mainly British resources. By this time the BEF could muster great numbers of men and firepower, although few of the 'the Old Contemptibles', of the original regular army, had survived. The British Force was mainly composed of the new volunteer army – enthusiastic but inexperienced. It is ironic that Kitchener was drowned in the *Hampshire* just three weeks before his army of recruits went into action.

For a week from 24 June, the German trenches were heavily bombarded by the British Fourth Army with an estimated 1.7 million shells. It was later learned that about one third were faulty and did not explode. Early on 1 July, wave after wave of British infantry, expecting little opposition, scaled the ladders of their trenches and carrying their 66 pounds of equipment, walked shoulder to shoulder across no-man's-land. To their horror they found that much of the barbed wire remained uncut and the machine gun posts and German dugouts were still largely intact.

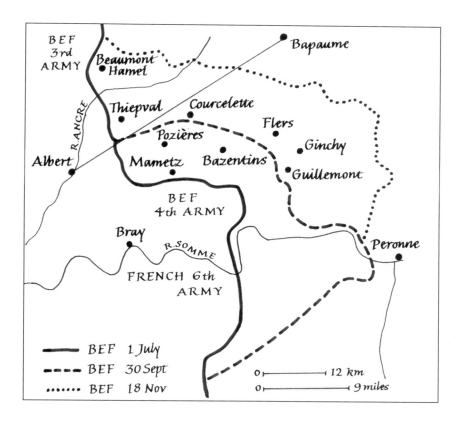

The Somme
1 July -
18 November
1916

As easy targets the British infantry were felled in thousands by machine gun fire. On the first day there were 57,000 casualties, more than a third of them fatal – the greatest loss suffered by the British army in a single day.

One young soldier, not from Alderbury but whose name is commemorated on his family's grave in Alderbury churchyard, fell on that first day of the battle. His name was Thomas Charles Pearman and he was in the 2nd Middlesex Regiment. He is not named on either of the Alderbury war memorials because the family was living elsewhere at the time of his death.

THOMAS CHARLES PEARMAN
S/6971 Private
2nd Battalion The Middlesex Regiment
23rd Brigade, 8th Division
Died 1 July 1916. Aged 18.

Thomas Pearman's family hailed from Middlesex and before that, from Alton in Hampshire. The family headstone in Alderbury churchyard also bears the names of his sister Edith Eleanor who died in 1921 aged 15, his

23

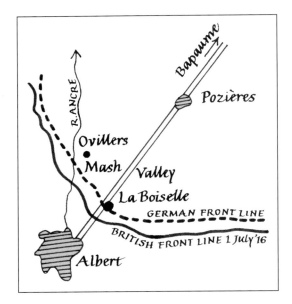

mother Rosalind Alice who died in 1934 and his father Thomas Holloway Pearman who died in 1936. Possibly his father came to work in the village and an 'in memoriam' notice[4] in a local newspaper states that the family was in Whaddon in 1921. In 1925 they were living in a house called Somme.[5] The deceased soldier's name may have been added to his sister's headstone at the time of her death in 1921. There were three other children, Emily, Annie and Frederick. There is a family connection to that of Pte Thomas Pearman Bundy – who died on the Somme in December 1916 – whose mother also from came from Alton.[6]

Mash Valley
1 July 1916

On 1 July, the beginning of the Battle of the Somme, the 2nd Middlesex was in the centre of the line just north of La Boiselle, by the Albert to Bapaume Road. At 7.35am the 23rd Brigade led by the 2nd Middlesex and the 2nd Devonshires, advanced in waves towards Pozières along the infamous Mash Valley between the villages of Ovillers and La Boiselle, two German strongholds. They suffered almost total annihilation by cross machine-gun fire from the two villages but about 70 men managed to get into the German trench and held 300 yards of it for two hours. They withdrew when the enemy counter-attacked on both flanks.

Pte Pearman was killed in action on that first day. He is commemorated at Ovillers Military Cemetery. It stands at the head of the former Mash Valley on what would have been the German front line at that time. The small road now running across the valley below marks the British front line. Thomas Pearman was awarded the British Medal and the Victory Medal.

For the next 142 days the enemy lines were relentlessly attacked and just as bitterly defended, yard by yard, across fields, woods and ridges, incurring huge casualties for both sides.

THE SOMME: GINCHY, 10 SEPTEMBER 1916

Pte Edward Hatcher of Whaddon, serving with the 1st Battalion Welsh Guards, had only been married for four days when on 8 August 1916, he was posted with his unit to Ypres in Belgium.

24

EDWARD HATCHER
1321 Private
1st Battalion Welsh Guards
Died 10 September 1916. Aged 28.

The 1901 census records that Edward Hatcher was born in Appleshaw, Hampshire, the son of Edward Hatcher, a retired police sergeant, and his wife Annie. The family lived at Pines Cottage, Whaddon. His elder brother John was also killed in the war and his younger brother William, who survived, served with the Wiltshire Regiment. When Edward enlisted in the Welsh Guards, in Brecon, at the age of 27, he was also a policeman. From 1 May 1915, Edward had three months training at the Guards depot in Caterham, Surrey and was then posted to the 2nd Reserve Battalion stationed at the Tower of London. He married Elizabeth Mary Williams at the Parish Church of Llyswen, Brecon on 4 August 1916. Four days later he joined the 1st Battalion Welsh Guards at Ypres before going to the Somme early in September. His destination was Ginchy, a small German-held hamlet east of Albert, that stood on high ground surrounded by woodland.

The battalion diary indicates that the march, via Carnoy, was notable for its road congestion, packed animals, accumulation of guns and the churned up state of the battlefield after months of shelling. A halt was called at Carnoy while the troops enjoyed a well-earned tea and dinner on the hillside. At 8pm they left with two days rations to move to the front as a relieving force. Guides met them at Bernafay Wood, the scene of much fighting a month earlier, and they were taken through the village of Guillemont which had been captured with terrible losses only days before. As they went through its ruins they met small parties of German soldiers who surrendered to them. It was pitch black when they arrived at Ginchy. Rifle fire was encountered from some enemy snipers occupying houses within the centre of the village. Orders were received that the four companies of Welsh Guards, together with Grenadier Guards, should take over the positions of the 47th and 48th Brigades situated north and east of the village.

The morning of 10 September at 7am was very misty and there was very little light. Communications during the night had failed but a returning patrol reported that it had located 70 men of the 48th Brigade in a sunken road to the east of the village. At that moment the enemy mounted a strong attack. The Welsh Guards fell back to a wood which was

The Battle of Ginchy, 10 September 1916

E. Hatcher headstone. Photograph courtesy of Trevor Hayward

a mass of deep shell holes, demolished houses, piles of earth from German dug-outs and fallen trees. In the mist it was difficult to distinguish friend from foe in the next shell-hole. Hand-to-hand fighting ensued until the enemy withdrew. However, just before noon, another advancing enemy battalion was observed and the battle continued fiercely all day. The artillery could do little to assist the close fighting inside the wood. At the end of the day Ginchy village was successfully taken but the losses were very heavy. Pte Edward Hatcher was one of the Welsh Guardsmen killed in the action.

He is commemorated at London Cemetery and Extension, Plot 9, Row E, Grave 21, Longueval, Somme. It is one of five cemeteries in the locality. The original London Cemetery started with the burial of men from the 47th Division in a large shell hole, during September 1916: other graves were added later. The Extension has over 3,869 casualties commemorated on this site from the 1914-18 war, with 3,114 of them unidentified. Edward was awarded the British War and Victory Medals.

THE SOMME: FLERS-COURCELETTE, 15 SEPTEMBER 1916

The first day of the major battle of Flers and Courcelette was the 15 September. These two villages are three miles apart, north-east of Albert and within the line between Combles and Thiepval. It was hoped that a victory here would aid an advance for the cavalry into the enemy-held town of Bapaume. The battle is especially remembered for the first use of tanks in warfare.

ARTHUR CECIL BUNDY
150829 Private
1st Canadian Mounted Rifles (Saskatchewan Regiment)
8th Brigade 3rd Canadian Division
Died 15 September 1916. Aged 23.

Arthur was born in 1893, the second son of Mrs Evelyn Bundy and the late Edward Bundy of 37 Silver Street, and brother of Ernest (killed at Ypres) and William (who survived the war). All three brothers served with the Canadian Corps. There were four sisters, Laura, Cecily, Lavinia and Winifred. Arthur joined up on 24 November 1915 at Brandon, Manitoba and lived at 338 1st Street, the same address as Wilfred Mouland who had enlisted in the same regiment only a few days before. In Arthur's attestation papers he is described as a farmer, unmarried, 5ft 6ins tall with dark brown hair and blue eyes. Attached at first to the 79th Battalion, he transferred to the 1st Canadian Mounties on landing in France on 7 June 1916. Arthur Bundy, probably with his friend Wilfred Mouland, joined his unit in the field two days later, shortly after his brother Ernest, of the same Canadian battalion, had been killed (on 5 June 1916). In late August the Canadian Corps left the Ypres Salient to play their part at the Somme in the Battle of Flers – Courcelette.

The Canadian sector was situated along the Pozières Ridge, the highest part of the area. Arthur Bundy's infantry battalion, the 1st CMR was deployed in front of an enemy-held farm situated in a dominant position on the ridge. Mouquet Farm (known by the British as 'Mucky Farm' and by the Australians as 'Moo-cow Farm') was a key to capturing the large village of Thiepval to the west. The highly fortified farm was the headquarters of a German brigade and its ruined buildings, deep stone cellars and underground tunnels were linked to a complex trench network. In August and early September nine attacks in the area by three Australian divisions had been repulsed at a total cost of 11,000 casualties. On 15 September the Canadians made another attempt to take the farm.[7] The order issued from

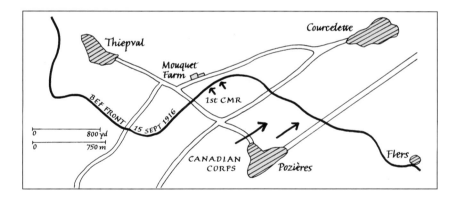

Pozières, Mouquet Farm, Thiepval, 15 September 1916

the Divisional HQ to the 1st CMR was to raid, occupy and take prisoners. The attack took place at 6.20am and a report in the divisional war diary described it as *'successful'*. The raiding party returned to their own lines at 7.30am with one prisoner, having lost 8 men killed and 16 wounded.

Among the casualties was Pte Arthur Bundy. He was reported missing on 15 September and afterwards confirmed as killed on that day. He is commemorated in Serre Road Cemetery No 1, V11. E10, Pas de Calais, France. There are nearly 2,500 casualties from the 1914 - 18 war on this site, many of whom were brought here from the battlefields of the Somme and the Ancre after the armistice. Nearly three-quarters are unidentified. Arthur was awarded the British and Victory medals.

Eventually, Mouquet Farm was by-passed and captured later in September with the help of one of the new tanks. Allied gains on the first day of this battle were more than twice those of 1 July with the capture of three large villages and the piercing of two of the enemy's main defensive systems.

THE END OF THE SOMME OFFENSIVE:
NOVEMBER – DECEMBER 1916

Although the German line was pushed back during the autumn of 1916, it had not broken. The offensive continued and conditions on the battlefield deteriorated after a very wet summer. The final push came in November 1916, with the Battle of the Ancre, a tributary of the River Somme. The British Fifth Army attacked Beaumont Hamel, just north of the river, and it was successfully taken. The Royal Naval Division captured Beaucourt-sur-L'Ancre, a village two miles away on the river, but at great cost. As the winter weather gathered momentum and more rain, sleet and snow made movement almost impossible, the Somme offensive was discontinued in the wilderness of mud and water-filled shell-holes. At most the line had advanced about seven miles. However, the Germans had been forced to divert manpower from other theatres of war enabling the French to avoid defeat at Verdun.

Two more Alderbury men died before the Christmas of 1916: Thomas Bundy of the Machine Gun Corps on 18 December from wounds and, two days later, John Hatcher of the 1st Hampshires was killed in action.

THOMAS PEARMAN BUNDY
10316 Private
2nd Infantry Brigade,
1st Division Machine Gun Corps
Died on 18 December 1916. Aged 28.

Thomas was born in Alderbury in 1888, the eldest son of Robert and Ellen Bundy. He was married to Winifred Anne Bundy of Lynwood Cottage, Laverstock. In the 1901 census Thomas, then aged 12, is recorded living at Alderbury Junction with his parents, his sister Vera and his younger brother Robert, killed in the war in 1918. Thomas enlisted in the 8th Battalion The Wiltshire Regiment (Pte 22069) a holding battalion based at Wareham, on the 30 August 1915. He was transferred to the Machine Gun Corps (MGC) early in 1916 and sent to train at Grantham. He then went to the MGC Depot at Camiers, in France, from where he would have been sent to join units in the field.

THE INFANTRY DIVISION OF THE MACHINE GUN CORPS

The MGC was a huge corps divided into Infantry, Cavalry, Motor and Heavy branches. The Infantry of which Thomas was a member, was by far the biggest section with some 60 battalions on the Western Front

All the main armies used the heavy machine gun from the beginning of the war. The weapon was positioned on a low mount and fired at a rapid speed, ammunition being fed in automatically at about 600 rounds a minute. The need to be more portable in order to keep up with the infantry produced a lighter gun, the Lewis, that could be fired from the shoulder. These became the weapons of the infantry machine gun sections.

From March 1916, MGCs were created at divisionel level to support brigade companies so that the heavy guns could be positioned at a site different from that of the infantry, for greater concentration of targeted, long-range, overhead firing. The MGCs suffered more than 600,000 casualties in the war.

The 2nd Infantry Brigade to which Thomas belonged (the name was changed to the No. 2 Machine Gun Company in July 1916), was formed in France in January 1916 and was part of the 1st Division of the MGC. It fought in almost every major action including the 1916 Somme battles.

It is not known exactly when or how Thomas received his fatal wound but during the autumn and early winter of 1916 his company was active in the area of Mametz Wood, Bazentin-le-Grand and High Wood, a few miles east and north of Albert. His unit war diary shows that about 50 casualties had been sustained in the earlier part of this period but during the whole of November and December only one man was recorded as being wounded. This happened on 28 November at Bazentin-le-Grand when a gun took a direct hit. Thomas may have been this casualty as his unit was deployed in that location and he is buried in a nearby village.

Mametz, The Bazentins and High Wood, December 1916

Pte Thomas Bundy is buried in the Bazentin-le-Petit Military Cemetery, C.3. The military cemetery was begun at the end of July 1916 and used as a front line cemetery until May 1917. Bazentin was in German hands until 14 July 1916 when British forces captured it, lost it again in April 1918, and regained it four months later. Thomas was awarded the British War Medal and the Victory Medal.

The second Alderbury man to lose his life at the Somme that December was Pte John Hatcher of the 1st Battalion, The Hampshire Regiment.

JOHN PHILLIP HATCHER
18919 Private
1st Battalion The Hampshire Regiment
Died 20 December 1916. Aged 27.

John was born in Andover in 1889, son of Edward and Annie Hatcher of Southampton Road, Whaddon. He enlisted with the Hampshire Regiment at Birmingham although he was domiciled in Salisbury. His elder brother, Edward, was killed while serving with the Welsh Guards in September 1916. His younger brother William survived the war serving with The Wiltshire Regiment. He also had a sister Annie.

From 2 November to 7 December 1916, Private John Hatcher found himself in good billets at Abbeville, situated near the mouth of the River Somme and out of the line. The days were occupied with training, marching, exercises and divisional and brigade competitions. Plenty of leave was allowed. Then from 7 December the battalion spent a week in a muddy camp further inland by the river at Bray-sur-Somme. A week later the battalion moved to the front at Priez Farm near Combles. This section had just been taken over from the French and was described in the Regimental History as: ......*hardly conforming to British standards of what a front should be.*

For the next four days they stayed there as brigade reserve. On 19 December they relieved the 1st East Lancashires in some muddy shell holes opposite the most westerly end of St Pierre's Vaast Wood. It was 500 yards from the enemy's front line. On 20 December the battalion's diary noted: *Weather fine and cold. Enemy's artillery decidedly active.*

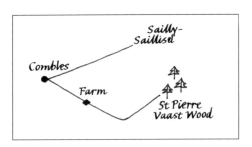

St Pierre Vaast Wood, December 1916

Pte John Hatcher lost his life that day – one of 15 men killed or missing during the two weeks the battalion spent near Priez Farm.

John lies at rest in the Sailly-Saillisel British Cemetery; V1.H.3, 10kms south of Bapaume, Somme. The cemetery was made after the armistice from small graveyards and isolated grave positions south and east of the two villages. There are nearly 400 casualties commemorated here. Of these nearly two thirds are unidentified. He was awarded the British War Medal and Victory Medal.

CHAPTER 3

THE GALLIPOLI CAMPAIGN 1915 – 16

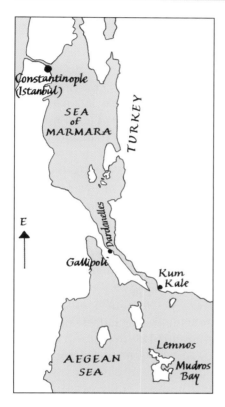

The first Alderbury man to lose his life in the Great War served in a campaign many miles from the Western Front. In August 1914 he was residing in Australia when he answered the call to arms. He joined the Australian Imperial Force destined to fight at Gallipoli against the Turks. His name was Edgar Mouland.

Constantinople, Dardanelles and Gallipoli

On 29 October 1914 Turkey forsook her neutrality and entered the war in support of the Central Powers, invading three Russian ports on the Black Sea. Turkey also closed the Dardanelles, the seaway that was a vital link between the Black Sea and the Mediterranean, thus preventing the passage of arms and food supplies between Russia and the Allies. Turkey's action was of great concern as it diverted Russian manpower from the war and threatened British interests in the Middle East, especially the Suez Canal. In February 1915 French and British warships bombarded Turkish forts at Kum Kale on the Asiatic side of the strait, followed in March by an attack using a fleet of old battleships that attempted to force a passage through to Constantinople. The action came too late and failed. The Turkish army had been retrained, revitalised and re-armed by Germany and the strait was defended and mined. Several British ships were sunk and the fleet turned away without achieving its objective.

In April 1915, a daring plan was devised to land an infantry force on Gallipoli, the peninsula on the European side of the strait. The Mediterranean Expeditionary Force, consisting of British, French, Indian and Anzac troops were assembled on islands in the Aegean Sea. A huge fleet waited to transport them as close as possible to secret landing sites where they would disembark into boats for the final landing.

EDGAR MOULAND
651 Lance Corporal
12th Battalion
3rd Infantry Brigade, 1st Australian Division
Died 25 April 1915. Aged 27.

Edgar Mouland was the son of John Mouland, an Alderbury blacksmith, and his wife Emma, of the Forge near The Green in Alderbury. His brothers were Bertram, also a blacksmith, Wilfred, who lost his life in France in 1917, and Reginald, who served with The Wiltshire Regiment. He had two sisters Mildred and Hilda. Edgar's attestation papers show that he enlisted on 7 September 1914 at Morphettville in South Australia. It is probable that he was already an emigrant to Australia as he was in the country within a month of Britain entering the war. From every state in Australia men had poured into recruitment offices to support Britain.

On enlistment, Edgar described himself as a motor driver and unmarried. He was 5ft 9ins tall with black hair and blue eyes. He was appointed to the 12th Battalion, 3rd Infantry Brigade of the 1st Australian Division and ten days later embarked at Melbourne on the transport ship *Geelong*. On 1 November the Australian and New Zealand Army Corps, (Anzac) set sail from Albany in Western Australia, the greatest fleet ever to cross the Indian Ocean. Aboard were 29,000 men, 12,000 horses - and apparently some pet kangaroos! They were bound for England but plans were changed en route and the fleet was diverted to Cairo in Egypt.

On arrival at Christmas 1914, the Anzac began intensive training at a camp in the desert near the Pyramids. On 2 March 1915 Edgar embarked on the ship *Devanha* at Alexandria. It was headed for the Aegean where Anzac battalions were to start their military campaign. It is most likely that the ship anchored at Mudros on the island of Lemnos, some 17 miles from the coast of Gallipoli, where Allied troops were amassing. Their objectives: to defeat the Turks on the peninsula, capture Constantinople and open up the Dardanelles. On 1 April 1915 Edgar was promoted to lance corporal.

In the early hours of 25 April, 75,000 men, 300 vehicles and thousands of animals were sent on their way to Gallipoli in a huge fleet of merchant ships. As the French created a diversionary attack on the opposite side of the strait, British troops landed at five beaches around Cape Helles at the tip of the peninsula. The Anzac troops were shipped 13 miles around the western coast to the cove at Gaba Tepe. Their orders were to seize the beach, advance inland to the ridge of Chunuk Bair, set up observation posts over the strait and cut off the enemy as they retreated from the British force at Cape Helles.

With the Australians in the vanguard, Edgar Mouland's 3rd Infantry Brigade reached the shallows just as dawn broke. Carrying their bayonets and heavy packs of equipment, the men leapt into the water and made for the beach under fire from the headland above. A nasty surprise awaited them. As it grew lighter it became apparent that the boats had brought them to the wrong location. Instead of a low sandy bank skirting the beach at Gaba Tepe with routes leading inland, they found themselves a mile further north in the cove of Ari Burnu under precipitous cliffs. The pathless scrub-covered ridges above them were dominated by that of Chunuk Bair, 250 metres high commanding views across the peninsular. As the Anzac tried to climb the cliffs under fire, men lost their bearings and separated from each other; while others fell on the rocks or down into hidden gullies and crevasses. Determined, many managed to clutch at roots and stones to haul themselves to the top. There they engaged in their first hand-to-hand bayonet combat. Some penetrated for about a mile or more into the hills. Edgar Mouland may have been one of these men, as he was last seen inland that afternoon.

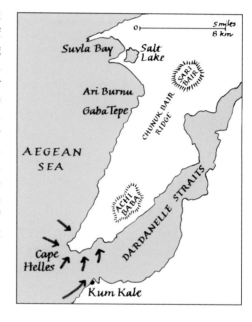

The Gallipoli Peninsula, April 1915

The Turks, only half a division strong, were unprepared for the landing in such an unexpected place. By mid-morning, faced with 14,000 Anzac that had come ashore along the coast, they began to retreat. It was sheer chance that brought an ambitious young Turk general, Mustafa Kemal, to the scene at that moment. (He was later to become 'Ataturk', leader of his nation). He rallied the men, brought in reinforcements and launched fanatical attacks all afternoon. By nightfall the Anzac were under siege, struggling to get back to the beachhead, with the wounded lying in hundreds among the rocks.

Edgar Mouland was reported missing. Months later, during a Red Cross enquiry, three witnesses from his company in the same charge that day, provided statements from their hospitals in Egypt and England. One stated that he had seen Edgar Mouland at about 9am on the morning of 25 April: two witnesses said that he had been seen about two miles back from the beach at 4pm in the afternoon. He was not seen again.

Edgar was one of 8,709 Anzac troops killed during nine months of campaigning in Gallipoli. The cove at Ari Burnu was renamed Anzac Cove and after the war it became a place of pilgrimage for Australians and New Zealanders who still commemorate Anzac Day on 25 April every year. L/Cpl Edgar Mouland is commemorated at Lone Pine Cemetery, Anzac, Turkey. The name derives from a single pine tree that grew on the spot.

After the war the original small cemetery was enlarged when scattered graves were brought in from the neighbourhood. Edgar was awarded the 1914 - 15 Star, the British Medal and the Victory Medal.

Early evacuation was refused by High Command who signalled that the troops must stay and 'dig, dig, dig' until they were safe. This they did – deep into the sides of the terrain (said to be the origin of the Australian nickname 'Digger'). They could not advance far inland nor would they be driven back to the sea. With daily casualties mounting they suffered the dust of the summer's stifling heat and the plagues of flies that brought sickness and dysentery. Then they endured the snow blizzards and flash floods of the worst winter for 40 years in which many perished from frostbite or drowning. A spirit of comradeship grew among them and an uneasy respect for their enemies sharing the same hardships.

In July 1915, the 5th Wiltshires came to Gallipoli with two Alderbury men, Pte Alfred Howe and Pte Harry Prewett. This was the first overseas campaign for the battalion, formed in 1914 from volunteers. After baptism in the trenches at Cape Helles, the 5th Wiltshire were sent to Anzac Cove to support landings at Suvla Bay, in the north of the peninsula. The battalion acquitted itself well capturing a vital ridge of hills during a night attack and holding the high ground. Then fortune turned against it. In the early hours of 10 August, with one company detailed to stay on duty, the remainder of the battalion was led up a steep and winding path to 'safe' dugouts at the head of a gully. The men bivouacked and disarmed to sleep. At dawn a division of Turks led by Mustapha Kemal came to the spot and fell upon them with bayonets. There was little chance of escape. Most ran straight into machine gunfire at the far end of the gully; a few climbed the sides and escaped over the top; some lay hidden at the bottom of a ravine among the dead and wounded – five of these were rescued exhausted and dehydrated 16 days later. The company on duty was outnumbered. A counter-attack failed and there were huge losses. Half the battalion was never seen again. The Commanding Officer and all his officers, except two, were killed. During the next few days small groups of men carrying the dead and wounded limped back to the beach[8]. It is not certain whether Alfred Howe and Harry Prewett were involved in this tragic incident but it seems probable. In any case, together with William Ingram (who was in another part of Gallipoli serving with the Royal Naval Division), they survived, only to fall at a later date in other theatres of the war.

The Gallipoli campaign was doomed to failure. In January 1916, High Command decided to risk complete evacuation from all the locations on the peninsula. In a magnificent operation of daring and subterfuge, this was achieved without a single casualty.

CHAPTER 4

THE MIDDLE EAST

MESOPOTAMIA (NOW IRAQ): 1915 -1918

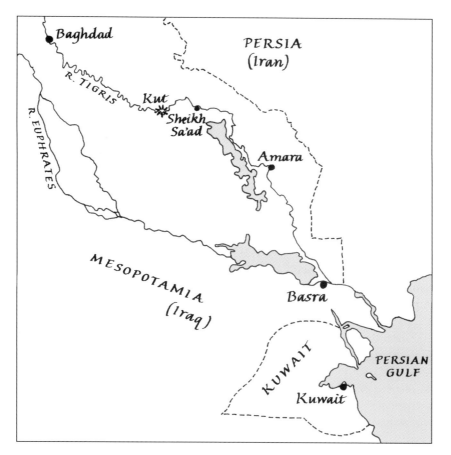

Mesopotamia

The alliance between the Turkish Ottoman Empire and the Central Powers in 1915 put at risk Britain's interests in the Middle East and endangered the strategic route to India. Recognising the vital importance of oil for future needs, Britain had obtained the Abadan Oil Field in 1913 in the neighbouring country of Persia (now Iran). In November 1914 British and Indian troops were posted from Bombay to Turkish-controlled Mesopotamia to protect oil installations. During 1915, with gunboats in support, they steadily advanced northwards from their base at Basra with the intention of capturing Baghdad. After successfully taking and passing the fortress town of Kut-el-Amara in September, the British found themselves under fierce counter-attack and had to retreat to Kut. From 5 December they were besieged and surrounded by 60,000 Turks. For the next 142 days they awaited rescue.

After their evacuation from Gallipoli, the remnants of the 5th Wiltshires badly needed reinforcements. Awaiting them at Mudros were 700 men from the 2nd and 3rd Battalions who had seen service in France. At the end of January 1916, in an attempt to rescue the besieged and starving British garrison, the battalion went via Port Said and Kuwait to Basra in Mesopotamia. After a period of training the men moved in barges along the River Tigris up to the Turkish front. Early in April the battalion fought its way through seven miles of Turkish entrenchment. Marshy ground and strong defences in open terrain protected Kut and the way was still barred. The battalion had to withdraw under heavy fire sustaining 293 casualties. Altogether, the British lost more than 4,000 lives in the rescue attempt. The garrison at Kut was forced to surrender on 29 April, after running out of food and water. The weakened and dehydrated survivors were taken prisoner and marched off to prison camps in the north of the country in the full heat of summer. This, plus fevers and neglect, accounted for the deaths of more than a third of them.

After the failed rescue attempt the 5th Wiltshires, numbering only 426, remained near Amara, on the banks of the River Tigris. Among its ranks were two veterans of Gallipoli, Pte Alfred Howe and Pte Harry Prewett.

ALFRED HOWE
9561 Private
5th Battalion, The Wiltshire Regiment
Died 17 June 1916.

Alfred Howe was born in Fisherton and enlisted at Salisbury. He was married to Mary Prewett and they lived in Alderbury. Many older residents will remember his nephew, Jack Howe, his wife and their son Tony who lived in Cherry Tree Cottage at the corner of Old Road and Clarendon Road. Pte Alfred Howe served in Gallipoli with the 5th Wiltshires and then in Mesopotamia as described above.

On the day that Pte Alfred Howe died, 17 June 1916, the battalion was holding a defensive position at Sheikh Saad, north of Amara. It was depleted in numbers due to many men being hospitalised suffering from heat exhaustion and dysentery. The summer temperature had reached 120 – 130 degrees Fahrenheit. During the month of June, 163 men had been sent to hospital. As the battalion had not been involved in any recent action, it is probable that Pte Howe died from an illness. His family were told that Alfred was receiving treatment at a hospital for pneumonia when it was overrun by the enemy and used for their own casualties. It has not been possible to corroborate this information. Alfred is buried at Amara and commemorated on panel number XV.G.1. His is one of the 4,621 burials from World War 1 here. In 1993 all the head stones were removed as salts in the soil were causing damage. A wall was erected containing the inscribed names of those buried in the cemetery. Alfred was awarded the 1914 – 15 Star, the British War Medal and the Victory Medal.

The 5th Wiltshire Battalion was in action again later that year, in December 1916, when it moved back to a position near Kut. In the New Year of 1917 it successfully attacked the Turkish front line and by early spring had crossed the River Tigris, only 40 miles from Baghdad. The battalion diary records that on 7 March they had camped south of Diala and were planning how to cross the river, a feat that other parties ahead of them had failed to do. Three nights later, in the dark and under the noses of the Turks only 400 yards away on the opposite bank, the entire battalion quietly ferried across in pontoons, incurring only one casualty. By daylight they had taken 120 prisoners and were on their way to Baghdad. The 5th Wiltshires were the first to enter the city as the Turks retreated. The citizens lined the streets and greeted the troops with great enthusiasm wherever they went. The battalion continued to advance northwards, clearing the villages of snipers and receiving gifts of eggs and oranges from friendly inhabitants as they passed.

HARRY PREWETT
9463 Private
5th Battalion, The Wiltshire Regiment
Died 29 March 1917. Aged 23.

Harry Prewett was born and brought up in in Alderbury, the youngest son of Henry James Prewett, a groom, and Louisa Prewett. His brothers were Oliver, William, Albert and Frederick, (who also served in The Wiltshire Regiment) He had two sisters, Emily and Amy. At the time of the 1901 census the family was living in one of the 'new' cottages near the steps between Southampton Road and Old Road. Harry enlisted on 17 August 1914 with the 5th Wiltshire Battalion at Devizes. He served in Gallipoli and Mesopotamia, as described above.

On 29 March 1917, the 5th Wiltshires, in pursuit of the Turks, were positioned along the Narwhan Canal, 35 miles north of Baghdad and two miles south of the Turkish front line at Marah. As the battalion advanced under heavy fire, there was no covering protection and they sustained casualties totalling 28 killed and 139 wounded. Harry Prewett was killed in action that day. During the night the enemy evacuated their positions and later the battalion was congratulated by the Brigadier General for a magnificent advance. Pte Harry Prewett is commemorated on the Basra Memorial, Iraq. He was awarded the 1914 - 15 Star, the British War Medal and the Victory Medal.

A few months later, in the early autumn of 1917, a farmer's son from Whaddon serving with 2/6th The Devonshire Territorial Battalion, arrived in Mesopotamia from garrison duty in India. He was Pte Hugh Tozer.

HUGH HENRY TOZER
65046 Private
2/6th Battalion, The Devonshire
Regiment
136th Brigade, 45th Division
Died 22 November 1917.
Aged 20.

Hugh Henry Tozer was born in Salisbury. He was the son of Thomas William and Annie Meaby Tozer who lived at Whaddon Farm (now known as Matrons' College Farm). Hugh enlisted at Salisbury into the 2/6th Battalion of the Devonshire Regiment.

The 2/6th Battalion was a Territorial Force formed at Barnstable in September 1914. Until July 1917, the battalion served in India, on garrison duty in Bombay, in the hills of Chakrata and at Peshawar. It was here that Private Hugh Tozer joined it. The battalion received orders to embark for Palestine but these orders were cancelled and instead the battalion was posted to Mesopotamia where two other Devonshire battalions were already serving. It arrived at Camp Magil, Basra, in September 1917, continued on to Amara and then moved upstream to Sheikh Sa'ad, on the banks of the River Tigris. Here the men lived in a tented camp and prepared to defend the position.

The battalion diary indicates that an unexciting spell on lines of communication duties was expected but Hugh Tozer died on 22 November 1917. The battalion had a number of deaths from an epidemic of influenza at that time and although the names of the casualties are not recorded, there is the possibility that Pte Hugh Tozer may have been among them. He is buried at Amara War Cemetery, I X11 H.10. He was awarded the British War Medal and the Victory Medal.

After the capture of Baghdad in 1917, described above, the 5th Wiltshires stayed in Mesopotamia keeping the pressure on the retreating Turks. During 1918 they spent their time training, repairing roads and building shelters. After April 1918 the battalion sustained no further casualties from enemy action. In September, to help with the capture of Mosul at the centre of the country's oil fields, the battalion advanced towards and took the town of Kirkuk. Hostilities were brought to an end on 1 November when the Turks signed an armistice. Pte Hedley Rolls was serving with the 5th Wiltshires at this time.

HEDLEY ROBERT ROLLS
9694 Private
5th Battalion The Wiltshire Regiment
(formerly 2nd Battalion)
Died 21 December 1918. Aged 33.

Hedley Rolls was born in 1885 and brought up in Alderbury, the second son of a large family. His parents, George and Elizabeth Rolls, lived in Vicarage Lane. He had an older brother Alfred, (who served on the Home Front with the Devonshire Regiment), and two younger brothers, Reynold, (who died in captivity in Germany), and William, (who was a driver with the Royal Field Artillery and survived the war). There were five sisters, Elizabeth, Ada, Alice, Una, and Ursula. Hedley Rolls volunteered on 24 August 1914 and was attached to the 2nd Wiltshires at Salisbury. This was a regular battalion that fought in the 1st Battle of Ypres.

Hedley must have been one of the early drafts of the 'new' army that joined the 2nd Battalion in France during 1915 as he was awarded the 1914 – 15 Star, given only to those who had served abroad before the end of that year. It is recorded that he transferred to the 5th Wiltshires in 1916, so he may have been among the 750 reinforcements from the 2nd Battalion that joined the depleted 5th on their way to Mesopotamia, after the evacuation of Gallipoli.

In 1918, during the closing weeks of the war in Mesopotamia, there was concern about malarial fever. Quinine was administered to all troops in an effort to stem the increasing number of sufferers. An epidemic of Spanish influenza also broke out that autumn but there were no reported deaths in the battalion from that source.

Pte Hedley Rolls served throughout the war from 1914 until after the armistice and it is tragic that after four years of conflict he died in December 1918 after hostilities had ceased. Probably he succumbed to one of the diseases of that inhospitable climate. He is buried in the Baghdad War Cemetery (North Gate) Iraq. He was awarded the 1914 – 15 Star, the British War Medal and the Victory Medal.

*Palestine
1917*

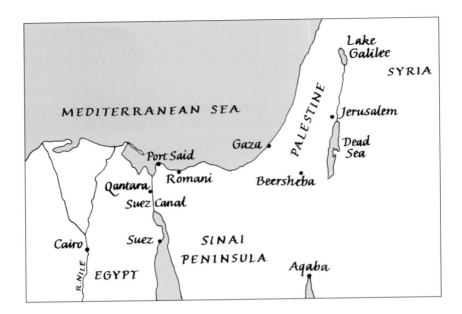

PALESTINE 1915 – 18

At first the main objective of the British Force in Egypt was to defend the Suez Canal so that Anzac and Indian troops could travel to the Western Front without hindrance. But in January 1915, the Turks attacked the Suez Canal from the Sinai Desert, attempting to cross it. They were beaten off and as the news from other theatres of war was discouraging, the British policy became one of defeating the Turks in the Middle East and removing Germany's ally from the war. In 1916 the British Forces of the Egyptian Expeditionary Force (EEF) advanced 100 miles to the east, removing the Turks from the Sinai Peninsula and establishing defensive positions along the borders of the Turkish province of Palestine. The Turkish Commander prevented any further advance by occupying the coastal fortress of Gaza and the line to Beersheba. In March 1917 an attack on Gaza was launched but despite the Turks being outnumbered by two-to-one, they held firm, and water shortages forced the EEF to retreat. In April a second attempt was made and again repulsed with high losses. In June 1917 General Sir Edmund Allenby took over the command of the EEF, charged with capturing Jerusalem by Christmas. The Third Battle of Gaza was launched on 31 October 1917 and this time, by first capturing the water supply at Beersheba, the battle was won. The EEF pursued the retreating Turks, breaking through their defences. General Allenby arrived in triumph at Jerusalem on 11 December 1917, as Turkish forces abandoned the city.

On consecutive days that November, two men from Alderbury lost their lives fighting in the Third Battle of Gaza.

CHARLES ERNEST ALBERY

201813 Private
1st /4th Battalion, The Wiltshire Regiment
Died 2 November 1917. Aged 24.

Charles Ernest Albery was the son of Charles
Albery of New Brompton, Kent and husband
to Hannah (nee Dummer) of Cockington,
Sussex. He was the only brother of Dorothy,
Win, Flo, Edith and twins Amy and Maisie. The
family lived at 'Tanglin', Firs Road, Alderbury in
a house built around 1914 – 15. The family kept
their own cows and his sister Maisie delivered milk
around the village on her bicycle.

In September 1917 Pte Charles Ernest Albery, serving
with the 1st/4th Wiltshires, left Bombay in India and set sail for Palestine to
join the EEF in its campaign to oust the Turkish Army from Gaza. A five-

Postcard sent home from India by Charles Albery.
It says: Dear Flo,
I went down Chaubattia Bazaar the other day with
R. England of Alderbury. A photo walla happened to
take a photo of bazaar and here we are. You will
notice I have grown a moustache. Perhaps Dad will
take this up and show it to Mr England the haulier. I
daresay he would like to see it. Ron is not sending
one home. This is for your album.

British War Medal and the Victory Medal awrded to Pte Charles Ernest Albery

hour journey took the battalion across the desert to the large camp at Qantara on the east bank of the Suez Canal, where they spent three weeks doing intensive training. On 14 October the battalion moved upline to the front at Lees Hill, a seven-mile march across sand. The heat, dust and a dire shortage of water made life uncomfortable and on the way the men witnessed smashed villages, deserted trenches and the gruesome relics of previous battles. The front line overlooked a deep wadi (a dry river bed) that commanded a view over enemy trenches, observation posts and hills. Behind stood the battered town of Gaza surrounded by palm trees. A mile beyond that was their eventual target – the imposing hill of Ali Muntar. Although their trenches were under continuous shellfire, forays were made into enemy territory. There were many casualties resulting from the Third Battle of Gaza but it ended with the capture of the ruined and deserted city on 7 November.

Pte Charles Ernest Albery was killed in action during the battle on 2 November 1917. He is commemorated at the Gaza War Cemetery where there are more than 3,000 casualties named from the 1914 – 18 war. He was awarded the British War Medal and the Victory Medal.

ERNEST HENRY HATCHER
202197 Private
2nd/4th Battalion The Dorsetshire Regiment
Died 3 November 1917. Aged 28.

Ernest Henry Hatcher was the son of Samuel and Alethea Hatcher of Alderbury, brother to Clara, Alice, Ethel and Olive. He married and resided at 29 Milford Hill, Salisbury with his wife Ellen (Cook) and their young son, Ernest Edward. According to family information, his father worked in William Hickman's shop on the Alderbury High Street and played in the village band with his brothers, Arthur (who was the band leader), Jake and Henry. Ernest went to Alderbury School and later, it is believed by the family, was employed by the Longford Estate. He enlisted at Salisbury but he may already have been a Reservist in the Wiltshire Territorials (Pte 4180). His wife, Ellen, worked as a domestic servant at

Godolphin School, a situation to which she returned when war widowed. *Alderbury*
His niece, Mrs Beryl Parry, writes that her mother told her that Alethea *band*
and Samuel watched for the day of Ernest's return and were absolutely *pre 1914*
devastated to learn of his untimely death by 'friendly fire'. Both Cook and
Hatcher families were very supportive of Ellen and her young son. Mrs
Parry remembers visiting her aunt and taking fresh vegetables from her
father's, (EH Parfitt), garden.

The 2/4th Dorsets served in India before being sent to Suez, arriving
on the 29 August 1917. The men entrained at Qantara before moving north
to Belah to prepare for the Third Battle of Gaza. At 8.40pm, on the evening
of 3 November, while patrolling the wadis and acting as listening posts,
one of the companies was attacked by an estimated 300 – 400 Turks under
cover of artillery barrage. They were successfully driven off with rifles,
Lewis guns, machine guns and artillery fire. The enemy kept up the barrage
and attacked again about three hours later with the same result. Patrols
were sent out to repair the wire, which had been cut in many places. The
casualties that night amounted to four men killed and five wounded. The
family learned later that Ernest had been killed in an accident of 'friendly
fire' in which he was shot in the legs. Unusually, the battalion war diarist
recorded the names of the four soldiers who died that night, including that
of Ernest Hatcher, but the circumstances of the accident were not
recorded. Pte Ernest Hatcher is commemorated at the Gaza War Cemetery,
XXXII. E.9. He was awarded the British War Medal and the Victory Medal.

CHAPTER 5

THE WESTERN FRONT 1917

FRANCE: SOMME, JANUARY – FEBRUARY 1917

1917 started as the old year had ended on the Western Front, with bitterly cold weather. During this coldest winter on record, an Alderbury serviceman returned to duty near the ruined village of Beaucourt, in the northern part of the Somme region. He had recovered after a long period of illness sustained during his time at Gallipoli. He was William Ingram of the Drake Battalion of the Royal Naval Division.

THE ROYAL NAVAL DIVISION

The Royal Naval Division (RND) was originally Winston Churchill's idea to mobilise the thousands of surplus men who flocked to join the Royal Navy in 1914, in an infantry role ashore. It consisted of seamen, marines and Kitchener's volunteers. Many came from the Royal Naval Volunteer Reserve (RNVR) founded in 1903 for offficers and ratings who undertook naval training in their own time. The division attracted men from many walks of life – academics, poets, authors, artists and the working class. The RND had three brigades. The battalions of the 1st and 2nd brigades were named after famous naval heroes – Collingwood, Hawke, Benbow, Drake, Howe, Anson, Hood, and Nelson. The Royal Marine Light Infantry battalions, named Portsmouth, Plymouth, Chatham and Deal (from September, 1914), made up the third brigade. The RND played a valiant role at Antwerp in October 1914, at Gallipoli in 1915 and in France and Belgium after that. In 1916 the Division was transferred from the Admiralty to the Army and renamed the 63rd (Royal Naval) Division but the men still proudly retained the traditions, rankings and parlance of the Royal Navy[9]. Two Alderbury men died fighting with the RND.

WILLIAM INGRAM
London Z/181 Able Seaman (RNVR)
Drake Battalion, RND
Died 4 February 1917. Aged 24.

William (Will) was the youngest son of George and Anna Ingram and brother to Bertie, Florence, Daisy, Dora and Freda. The family lived at Fort's Farm (now called Alderbury Farm) on Witherington Road, Alderbury. At the time of the 1901 census they were living at Whaddon Cottage and George Ingram, his father, was employed as a carter. Will Ingram joined the RNVR on the 14 December 1914. When enlisting he described himself as a farmer in the employment of Mr Barnard of Beckenham, Kent. He was initially attached to the Benbow Battalion but on the 12 June 1915 he transferred to the Drake Battalion serving on the Gallipoli Peninsula. In October, suffering from jaundice, he was sent by field ambulance to the Canadian hospital in Mudros on the island of Lemnos. Three months later he was sent home to England on the hospital ship *Aquitania* and admitted to Haslar Hospital in Portsmouth. On 21 December 1916 he rejoined Drake Battalion, now in the Somme, where the much-depleted Naval Division was at rest camp after a heroic performance during the Battle of the Ancre. This had cost the division nearly a third of its strength. The battle had ended with the capture of Beaumont Hamel and Beaucourt, two of the original 1 July targets.

On the bitterly cold nights of 18 and 19 January 1917 the men of the RND rejoined the line in front of Beaucourt village. Working their way forward and uphill, the infantry used isolated, frozen shell-holes for cover, digging not being possible in the frozen ground. Men bringing rations to these outposts could only move about at night and they were subjected to continuous shelling. Artillery and reserve companies fared little better. Rations were inadequate for the cavalry horses and the severity of the conditions proved too much for many of them.

On the first day of February, Drake Battalion moved up to the front line. From 6am the next morning and all during the day, enemy aeroplanes and artillery were active. On 3 February, Drake went into reserve in Beaucourt Trench with two of the companies deployed at the front, one at the casualty clearing station and the other deployed as carrying parties.[10] At 11pm the British artillery opened a heavy barrage on two enemy strongholds, Pusieux Trench and River Trench, some 300 yards and 400 yards away.

The events that happened that night are described in the diary of Arthur Asquith, the youngest son of Britain's former Prime Minister and an officer with the Hood Battalion.[11] Asquith recalls that on the frosty moonlit evening of 3 February, companies of the Hood and Hawke mounted a surprise

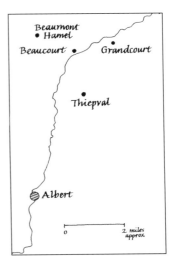

River Ancre Valley

Thiepval Memorial: photograph courtesy of Trevor Hayward

night attack on the two trenches. The Commanding Officer leading the Hood was injured and the attack became seriously disoriented, swinging in the wrong direction and leaving dangerously wide gaps. Attending as an observer, Asquith took command himself, managing to correct the situation despite getting shot in the arm. An action that was supposed to take only minutes turned into a 50-hour battle incurring heavy casualties. Will Ingram's battalion was sent up into the line early the next morning in support. He died of a wound on 4 February, possibly during this action. His name is commemorated at the Thiepval Memorial, Pier and Face 1A, Somme. He was awarded the 1914 – 15 Star, the British War Medal and the Victory Medal.

FRANCE: VIMY RIDGE, APRIL 1917

In the spring and the early summer of 1917, two Alderbury men Pte Wilfred Mouland and Sgt Walter Bundy died serving with a Canadian Corps that was rapidly earning a tough reputation. The Battle of Vimy Ridge was destined to become a famous victory that brought great national rejoicing and enduring pride to Canada, and the congratulations of the King himself. Within scarcely a day, the formidable Hindenburg Line was breached and the ridge won. It came at cost of 10,602 casualties including 3,598 fatalities, of whom Pte Wilfred Mouland was one.

WILFRED MOULAND
151074 Private
1st Canadian Mounted Rifles (Saskatchewan Regiment)
8th Brigade, 3rd Division
Died 7 – 10 April 1917. Aged 23.

Wilfred Mouland was the son of Emma and John Mouland. His brothers were Edgar (killed in Gallipoli), Reginald, Ralph, Claude and Bertram. His sisters were Mildred, Maud, Mona, Elsie and Hilda. At the time of the 1901 census, Wilfred was living with his parents and some of his siblings at the Forge, Alderbury. Sometime after the death of her husband in 1913, his mother moved to Nether Wallop. Wilfred went to Canada and enlisted on 13 November 1915 at Brandon, Manitoba, where he was living at 338 1st Street. In his attestation papers he is described as a blacksmith, unmarried, 5ft 5ins tall with grey eyes and dark brown hair. Among his papers there is a transcription of a letter to his mother, written while in Brandon. He wrote:
I have sent money home, it is not much but I have lived pretty well and you can't save money and have a good time too, out in this country but it may come in handy if I get shot up.

He embarked on the *SS Lapland* arriving back in England on 5 May 1916. Shortly afterwards he trained at the grenade school at East Sandling. This expertise was particularly important to the infantry as a grenade in the hands of a novice could be lethal to everyone around. In June he was attached to the 1st Canadian Mounted Rifles (1st CMR) and landed in France He joined his unit at Ypres on 9 June when the Canadians were successfully retaking the ground they had lost earlier in the spring.

The Canadian Corps remained at Ypres until the beginning of September holding the position and harrying the enemy. Then it moved to the Somme area to take part in major battles already described. At the end of October, most of the Corps, including the 1st CMR, moved north to Arras and the winter was spent in recuperation, training and strengthening defences while holding the line.

Between 23 February and 5 April 1917, the Germans secretly withdrew their armies to a newly-built front, known to the Allies as the Hindenburg Line, that stretched from Arras to Soissons. This was a deep, triple-zoned, self-supporting defence system, heavily fortified and wired. It was thought by the Germans to be impregnable. Undaunted, the new French commander, General Nivelle, continued with his plans for the Second Battle of the Aisne to be launched between Soissons and Reims using 1.2 million French troops. He rashly predicted a certain victory that would smash German defences, at little cost to his armies. To deflect German artillery from the area of the French battlefield, three British armies gathered on the northern flank, around Arras, and prepared for their own subordinate battle.

For the first time all four Canadian Divisions were assembled together for a simultaneous attack in front of the western slopes of Vimy Ridge, north of Arras. Vimy Ridge, a nine-mile stretch of high ground consisting of hilltops, fields and woodland, dominated the area between the rivers Scarpe and Souchez. Possession of the ridge was hugely important to the Germans as it was an excellent observation platform with natural defences and it barred the route to their factories and mines on the Douai Plain. It had defied earlier attempts at capture.

Position of the Canadian Corps at Vimy Ridge, April 1917

The 7,000-yard Canadian front was opposite the village of Vimy, on the eastern side of the ridge. In the weeks prior to the battle, roads and tramways were constructed to transport ammunition to the front and bring casualties speedily back; reservoirs were dug and pipes laid to provide water for the troops and 50,000 horses. Miles of underground cables were sunk deep into the earth for communications and, in a great feat of engineering, tunnelling companies excavated 11 electrically lit subways leading to the Canadian front. All work was done secretly under the cover of darkness. The officers were rehearsed meticulously in the details of timed targets denoted by black, red and blue lines using a full-scale replica of the ridge. Intelligence was updated frequently from aerial reconnaissance. On 20 March, a two-week bombardment began with daily machine gun fire and nightly raids by patrols.

On 8 April 1917, Easter Sunday evening, 50,000 Canadian infantry in numerical order of division, assembled in lines delineated by stakes marked with luminous paint. Two brigades from each division formed the first wave, each supported by a machine gun company. The remaining brigades were placed in reserve, to support as required. The weather was cold, threatening snow. The men had each been given a hot meal and a ration of rum and they waited in strict silence knowing that they were required to gain the whole crest of the ridge. Some companies crept into shell holes and ditches under fire, ready for the assault. The first objectives needed to be secured early and complete surprise was an essential element of the plan.

The attack opened at dawn on Easter Monday with the thunderous roar of 938 guns. As snow and sleet swept across the ridge, the 21 battalions moved forward into the attack.

Pte Wilfred Mouland's battalion, 1st CMR, 8th Brigade of the 3rd Division, attacked to the right of the front, opposite the Bois de la Folie. The ground was difficult to negotiate with muddy shell-holes, shattered trenches and torn barbed wire. However, the Canadian official historian records that their advance encountered only light resistance in the first phase, the enemy defences having been destroyed by the heavy artillery. The men reached the crest, the black line, on time at 7.30am and occupied the western edge of Bois de la Folie. After a scheduled rest, they moved on to the red line, their final objective, which they reached albeit with heavier fighting as resistance mounted. By the end of the day, three of the four Divisions had reached their goals and the 7,000-yard front, to a depth of 4,000 yards, had been taken and consolidated. The ridge was never to change hands again. [12]

Pte Wilfred Mouland was killed sometime between 7 and 10 April. He is buried in Cabaret-Rouge British Cemetery, Souchez, Pas de Calais, France XIV. M.2. He was awarded the British War Medal and the Victory Medal.

Souchez lies on the road to Bethune. The Cabaret-Rouge was a house just outside the village. Nearby, the British cemetery was begun in March 1916 and the British headquarters were in dugouts opposite. The cemetery was used until August 1917, mainly for casualties of the Canadian and 47th London Divisions. There were a further 7,000 casualties brought here after the armistice from the Arras battlefield.

WALTER JOSHUA BUNDY
1442 Sergeant
13th Battalion, Canadian Infantry (Quebec Regiment)
3rd Brigade (Royal Highlanders), 1st Division
Died 5 June 1917. Aged 25.

Walter was born in Alderbury in 1892, the son of Samuel and Charlotte Bundy of Church House, situated next to Alderbury Church. This is now known as Court House but then it was let to families of Longford Estate workers. In his attestation papers, signed in Ottawa on 28 July 1915, he describes himself as a fireman of 22 years 10 months, 5ft 7ins tall, unmarried with brown hair and grey eyes. Walter set sail from Canada for England in June 1916 on the *SS Missanabie*, arriving at Liverpool in July. He was assigned to the 73rd Battalion at Bramshott from where he embarked for Le Havre on 11 August. Two months later he was promoted to lance corporal. In December he underwent training in the use of grenades. Further promotion came in March 1917 when he became a sergeant in the 73rd battalion, part of the 4th Division, one of the four Canadian divisions involved at Vimy Ridge.

In the battle of Vimy Ridge the 4th Canadian Division had the most difficult target of taking the summit of Hill 145, the highest and most important ground. Surprise tactics did not succeed as the defences around the hill were very strong. The 12th Brigade, including Sergeant Bundy's 73rd battalion, made an encouraging start and consolidated the left flank but others ran into difficulties and fighting in front of the hill continued all day in a snowstorm. The hill was finally captured the next day. Walter Bundy survived that battle and a few days later he was transferred to the 13th Battalion of the 1st Division.

The much-vaunted French offensive on the Aisne, launched on 16 April, had failed disastrously by the beginning of May, incurring enormous French casualties. Mutiny became widespread among the demoralised French soldiers. A new Commander-in-Chief, General Petain, replaced General Nivelle and restored discipline. With the abandonment of the Second Aisne battle and with the French army in some disarray for the time being, the British Command turned its attention back to Belgium, determined to break through German lines around Ypres with an attack at

Messines Ridge based on the Canadian strategy at Vimy. In consequence, one army and most of the heavy artillery was transferred to Flanders. In the meantime, attacks were resumed in the area between the River Souchez and the River Scarpe aimed at disguising British intentions and engaging German manpower. On 3 May the 1st Canadian Division took part in a fierce battle around the small hamlet of Fresnoy, which was taken but lost again after the division went into reserve.[13] On the first day of June, situated north of Fresnoy, Sgt Bundy's 13th Battalion was called into the front line again at Thelus Mill Cave. The first few days and nights were relatively quiet but early in the morning of 5 June, the enemy shelled a nearby railway and in an air attack, 30 - 40 bombs were dropped on and around Divisional HQ killing many officers and other ranks. On the front line Sgt Walter Bundy was a casualty, receiving a shell wound to his left groin. Dangerously injured he was carried to the 23rd Casualty Station where he died soon afterwards.

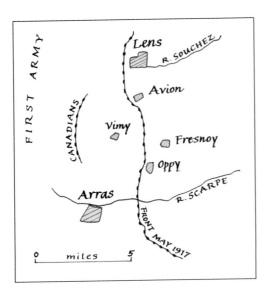

Battles of the Scarpe May - June 1917

He is buried in Lapugnoy Military Cemetery, Pas de Calais, Plot 1V. C. 9. Lapugnoy is a village six miles west of Bethune. There are now 1,500, 1914-18 war casualties buried on this site. Sgt Walter Bundy was awarded the British War Medal and the Victory Medal.

BELGIUM: YPRES, PASSCHENDAELE, JULY –NOVEMBER 1917

After a successful offensive at Messines Ridge, Belgium, in June, British High Command planned the Third Battle of Ypres, known as Passchendaele, launched on the 31 July 1917. The Ypres Salient, being the only part of Belgium still in Allied hands, was continually under pressure from the enemy. The Allies aimed to push out from Ypres, smash through the German Fourth Army and recapture the ports of Ostend and Zeebrugge, from where the German submarines and destroyers had been operating with devastating effect. The plan failed. The initial attack was successful but a month's preliminary bombardment by four million shells mutilated and destroyed the drainage system of the battle area. Torrential storms turned the land into a quagmire of knee-deep mud and water in which men and animals drowned. In these conditions the battle continued into the late autumn up to the Passchendaele Ridge, by which time only five miles of ground had been gained at a cost to both sides of a quarter of a million casualties. Pte Frank Harper of Alderbury was killed on the first day of the Battle of Passchendaele.

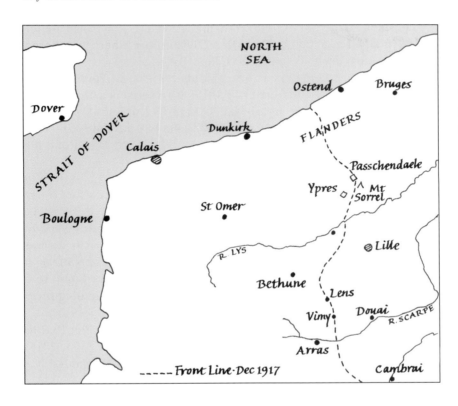

The Western Front December 1917

FRANCIS GEORGE HARPER
203065 Private
B Company, 2nd Battalion, The Wiltshire Regiment
Died 31 July 1917.

Francis (Frank) Harper was born in Amesbury and enlisted at Salisbury. He lived in Alderbury with his wife and two small sons, but their address is not known. Before being transferred to the Wiltshire Regiment in July 1916 he was in the 11th Battalion The Somerset Light Infantry (Pte 265920).

On 18 July 1917, a few days before the battle began, the 2nd Wiltshires proceeded via St Omer, to the Steenvorde area and encamped at Abeele. The battalion diary records that on Monday 23 July the Archbishop of York addressed the assembled battalions. Early on the morning of the 29 July the battalion occupied the trenches and until the evening of the 30th was targeted with gas shells. Pte Frank Harper's B Company suffered some casualties. It was still dark when B Company launched its own attack at 3.40am on the 31 July. The enemy put down a barrage on the front line trenches and considerable machine gun fire but within a few hours the company had achieved its objective with 40 prisoners taken and a new company headquarters established. Heavy shelling continued all day.

Pte Frank Harper was reported missing. It was later confirmed that he had been killed in action on 31 July 1917. He is buried at Hooge Crater Cemetery, Ypres (Ieper) Belgium XIII. F. 13

Hooge Crater Cemetery is four kilometres east of Ypres. A mine explosion had created the crater in 1915. The cemetery was begun in October 1917. There are nearly 6,000 1914-18 Commonwealth war casualties buried or commemorated on this site of whom over 3,500 are unidentified. Frank Harper was awarded the British War Medal and the Victory Medal.

In 1917 several events happened that affected the future conduct of the war. In May 1917, America finally declared war and joined the Allies although her troops were not to be operational for another year. In October, the Russian Revolution caused Russia to withdraw from the war releasing many German divisions from the eastern front to operations in the west and, in that same month, the Italians lost a major battle to a combined Austro-Hungarian and German army.

CHAPTER 6

GREECE AND ITALY 1915 – 1918

SALONIKA (NOW THESSALONIKA)

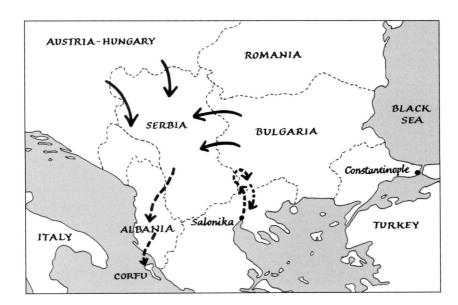

Salonika 1915, The Allies trapped at Salonika as the Serbs flee from enemy attacks from north and east

In August 1915, Bulgaria mobilised her army after signing a pact with Germany and Austria-Hungary to oppose Serbia. A month later, Greece allowed Allied troops to set up a base at the port of Salonika, neutral soil, and by October 150,000 British and French troops had arrived there intending to provide aid to the Serbs. However, they were too late. Germans and Austro-Hungarians from the north and Bulgarians from the east had attacked Serbia. Almost surrounded, the Serbian army escaped into the Albanian Mountains where many died of hunger and cold during the winter. The Allies could not help as a large Bulgarian force blocked their passage and so they had to turn back to Salonika. The remnants of the Serbian Army were eventually evacuated by Allied ships to the island of Corfu but later they rejoined the Allies at Salonika. By 1917 a total of 600,000 multinational troops were deployed there, including the Greeks, who had joined the Allied cause. In September 1918 a combined Allied offensive successfully forced the armies of the Central Powers to retreat. Allied casualties in the whole campaign amounted to 481,000, mainly caused by malaria.

CHARLES HAZEL BEAVEN
173546 Driver
Royal Engineers
Died 1 February 1917. Aged 26.

The spelling of the surname on the memorials has been corrected here.

Charles Hazel Beaven was born in Salisbury, the eldest son of Mr and Mrs C. Beaven of West Harnham. He married Mabel Etta and they lived at Ladies Cottages, Whaddon. A daughter was born to the couple only seven weeks before he died. Charles enlisted in Salisbury and was part of the General Base Depot for the British Salonika Force located at the port itself. His unit, Number 2 Section, was formed on 27th January 1917 and as a driver his main duties were to receive drafts of men and equipment and despatch them to companies in the field.

Disease was by far the biggest killer in this area of Greece, especially malaria. Driver Beaven's military death certificate specifies lobar pneumonia as the cause of his death. He is buried in Lembet Road Military Cemetery, Salonika, Greece, Grave number 793. He was awarded the British War Medal and the Victory Medal.

THE ITALIAN FRONT

With the promise of territorial gains in the event of victory, the Italian Government agreed to support the Allies against Austria-Hungary in April 1915. The fighting was concentrated in the mountainous areas of northern Italy, along the Trentino and Isonzo rivers and towards Trieste. For nearly two years the major powers allowed the two countries to battle it out with huge losses on both sides and neither gaining any permanent advantage. After the Eleventh Battle of Isonzo in September 1917, the Austro-

Hungarians, on the point of collapse, called on Germany for help. Germany responded with reinforcements and during the following month masterminded an attack at Caporetto. Taken by surprise, the Italians suffered a disastrous and humiliating defeat having to withdraw to the Piave River, only 30 kilometres from Venice. Concerned, the Allies sent British and French troops to support the Italians: among them was Private Albert Northeast of the 2nd Warwickshire Battalion.

ALBERT NORTHEAST
22080 Private
C Company, 2nd Battalion,
The Royal Warwickshire Regiment
Died on 3 August 1918. Aged 38.

Albert Northeast was the son of Edward, an estate labourer, and Jane Northeast of Alderbury. He was brother to Harriet, James, Ernest and Ellen. The 1901 census shows the family living in Rumbold's Lane in Frogham. (an area of Whaddon, near Rectory Farm). Albert, being 21 years old and independent, is not listed at the address. At the time of his enlistment, Albert was residing in Islington where he joined a London battalion (Pte 6561). He transferred later to the 2nd Battalion of The Royal Warwickshire Regiment, 7th Division. This was a regular division that served in France and Flanders. It suffered very heavy losses at Polygon Wood in the 3rd Battle of Ypres (Passchendaele). In November 1917, the 7th Division was one of five British and six French divisions selected to go to North Italy to support the demoralised Italian army after their huge defeat.

The 2nd Warwicks made the journey via the Riviera to Cera and then marched to Musano, ten miles behind the front. The Italians had managed to secure the line and the relative calm was a welcome change for the embattled troops fresh from the mud of Passchendaele. The next few weeks were spent in billets where they trained in hill fighting. On 18 January 1918, the battalion took over a line of trenches on the Montello, a steep embankment on the west bank of the River Piave. Patrols across the strong current of the Piave were adventurous and difficult and had to be made using the aid of a rope fastened from shore to shore. Anyone falling in could be washed downstream and drowned. In April 1918, the British moved to the Asiago Plateau in the mountainous district of the north with the 2nd Warwicks positioned in trenches at Monte del Busibollo. From here, a successful raid was held against the Austrians at Ambrosini. That apart, the Regimental History states:

The first nine months of 1918 were generally uneventful except for a brief period of the Austrian Offensive in June. The 2nd Warwicks were in billets during that skirmish and they were not called upon in the action.

*Northern Italy
Italian / Allied
Offensive
1918*

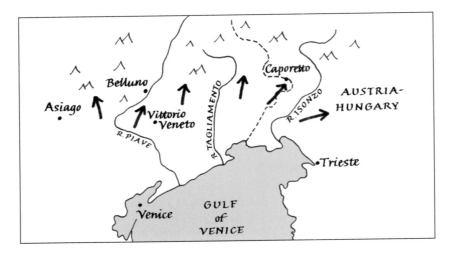

On the first day of August some companies moved into the front line and others formed working parties under the Royal Engineers. The weather was fine. Patrols went out day and night. At 2.30am on 3 August, a barrage was opened on the Austrian front. The enemy retaliated against the front line and the Warwickshire battalion headquarters. When the barrage stopped at 3.45am, two men from C Company had been killed and two wounded. One of those killed was Pte Albert Northeast.

He is buried at Boscon British Cemetery, Italy, situated on the Asiago Plateau near Vincenza. He was awarded the British War Medal and the Victory Medal.

At the end of October 1918, the Italians and the remaining five British and French divisions, won the decisive Battle of Vittorio Veneto, dividing the Austro-Hungarian forces in northern Italy. This effectively ended the war for them and fighting officially ceased on 3 November when an armistice was signed. The Austro-Hungarian Empire proceeded to break apart and separate republics of Austria and Hungary were created.

CHAPTER 7

THE WESTERN FRONT 1918

The beginning of 1918 saw German armies still in defensive positions entrenched behind the Hindenburg Line having repulsed the Allied offensives in the second half of 1917. As the Russians were now out of the war, the German Command was able to transfer many divisions from the eastern to the western front but with the North Sea blockaded, the countries of the Central Powers were desperately short of materials and food for both troops and civilians. Their U-boat campaign had failed to stop the flow of British ships travelling in convoys and protected from the air. Protest marches and strikes in Germany grew as starvation threatened the population. Casualty rates increased for all the warring nations and more and more conscripts were needed. Tentative peace negotiations failed to satisfy either side. The entry of America into the war with its vast resources made the German High Command realise that they must do something to win the war outright before America's full contribution took effect.

At the end of 1917, Alderbury's Frederick Hatcher was serving with the RND at Welsh Ridge on the Flesquières Salient, ground snatched from the Hindenburg Line during November 1917.

FREDERICK CHARLES HATCHER
R/5495 Able Seaman (RNVR)
Hawke Battalion (formerly of the Nelson Battalion)
Died on 21 March 1918. Aged 24.

Frederick Hatcher was born in 1894 and brought up in Alderbury, the son of Arthur and Laura Hatcher and brother to Percy (who served with the Middlesex Regiment), Edward (who served in the Royal Artillery), Felton, Elizabeth and Bertha. The family lived by Alderbury Bridge, Clarendon Road. In civilian life he was employed as a platelayer on the London South-West Railway. He enlisted in the Army Reserve in December 1915 but was not mobilised until 23 July 1917 when he enrolled with the RNVR. On 20 November he left England for Calais to join Nelson Battalion at Welsh Ridge near the medieval town of Cambrai, that had been held by the Germans since 1914.

Welsh Ridge on the Flesquières Salient was a vital area commanding approaches to two enemy centres which, if yielded, would give this hard-won section of the Hindenburg line back to the Germans. The Naval Division had been given the task of constructing a fortified, defensive line: not an easy task on these shattered slopes and with little in the way of

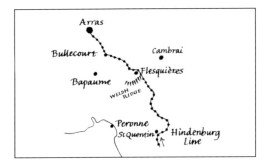

*Flesquières
Salient:
Welsh Ridge*

materials. At dawn on the 30 December 1917 the enemy struck against the whole of the British front, snow on the ground masking the first wave of camouflaged, white-clothed invaders. The crest of the ridge was lost and then won back again by the determination of Nelson and Anson battalions. In the desperate battles that followed, the valour shown by the Naval Division at Welsh Ridge against numerically superior forces has gone down in the annals of its history. They fought off the enemy's advances and substantially held their ground while incurring very heavy losses of 1355 men and 63 officers.[14]

Frederick managed to survive the battle and early in 1918 was one of hundreds of soldiers temporarily attached to the 7th Entrenching Battalion. This was one of the advance units to which infantry and engineers were posted to construct and repair trenches and roads. In the expectation of a German spring offensive, they worked furiously to complete defensive positions eight miles behind the front line. On 15 March, with a shortage of manpower, Nelson and Howe battalions were disbanded. Frederick was among 170 men transferred to Hawke Battalion engaged on repairing the wire along the front line of the Flesquières Salient. These new reinforcements made up C Company under the command of an officer of the Nelson and probably included Frederick Hatcher. His new battalion was under constant bombardment that had already cost it over 500 casualties, mainly gassed. The Hawke war diary for 16 March remarks: *"There is still a distinct smell of gas in this area."* Over the next three days 76 more troops were gassed.

THE MICHAEL OFFENSIVE, 21 MARCH 1918

During the winter of 1917-18 the German Military Command led by General Ludendorff and supported by the Kaiser, made secret preparations for a series of knock-out blows, known as Kaiserschlacht or The Kaiser's Battle, that would divide the French and British armies. They were scheduled to take place in the spring of 1918 and great care was taken to conceal the build up of men and artillery. The first of these offensives, code-named MICHAEL, entailed a 50-mile rapid advance from Arras to St Quentin and La Fère, across the old Somme battlefields. This was against the weakest and most overstretched zone defended by the British Third and Fifth Armies. A million German troops in three armies, commanded in the south of the area by Crown Prince Wilhelm and in the north by Prince

Rupprecht, would be supported by 6,000 guns and spear-headed by specially trained storm troopers.

At 4.40am on 21 March the MICHAEL Offensive began with a ferocious five-hour bombardment. The first attack came at 9.40am under cover of thick fog increasing the element of surprise. At the Flesquières Salient, the Hawke C Coy, guarding an outpost, lost 60 men killed or captured. Pte Frederick Hatcher was reported missing. As no further news was received it was assumed that he was killed on that day. He is commemorated on Bay 1 of the Arras Memorial for the Missing in the Faubourg-d' Amiens Cemetery, Pas de Calais commemorating almost 35,000 casualties of the British, New Zealand and South African Forces who have no known grave. He was awarded the British War Medal and the Victory Medal.

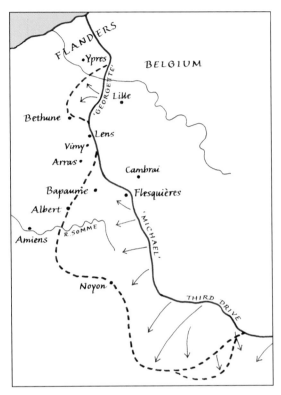

At that same time, the southern part of the British line near St Quentin was attacked where Pte Henry John Sims of Alderbury was serving with the 6th Battalion of the Somerset Light Infantry, part of Gough's Fifth Army.

German Offensives, Spring 1918

HENRY JOHN SIMS
29189 Private
A Company, 6th Battalion The Somerset Light Infantry
Died 21st March 1918. Aged 19.

Henry John Sims (John) is listed on both Alderbury memorials as John Sims. He was the son of policeman Harry Sims and his wife Emma who lived in Old Road, Alderbury. They lived there from 1916 until 1921 when they moved to the Police Station, Eastcott Road, Swindon, the address given on the CWGC entry.

His battalion, the 6th Somersets, had had a fairly quiet winter in 1918, encamped near St. Quentin, in the forward zone of the Fifth Army's 30-mile front between Flesquières and La Fère. The line was seriously under-manned having been extended in January to include 25 miles of the adjoining French front. Behind lay the area devastated by the German army in its scorched earth policy as it withdrew to the Hindenburg Line in the spring of 1917. For some weeks the Germans had deluged the British line with mustard gas, its fumes deadly and long-lasting. The battalion war diary describes the horrific events of the morning of 21 March:

> *At 4.30am the enemy opened an intense bombardment with all calibre shells, using a new kind of shell, the smell of which was not unpleasant, but had the effect of sleeping gas. At 8.30 am he finished gas shelling but continued with other shells. It was very foggy, extra sentries were posted at all points. All Signal communication was cut by 4.40 am. At 10.20 am news was received by runner, the enemy was in the front line........fighting immediately commenced. 2 Pigeons were immediately despatched & papers all burnt, the enemy at 10.30 am was streaming down the St Quentin Road from both flanks and poured into La Folie Quarry....*

The battalion's casualties in the Battle of St. Quentin, those actually in the front line at the time of the attack, amounted to 20 officers and 540 other ranks. Henry John Sims was one of the fatalities. He is named on the Pozières Memorial to the Missing, Panel 25 and 26. The memorial takes the form of a wall surrounding a cemetery and it is dedicated to the men of the Fifth and Fourth Armies who have no known grave. It relates to the period of the final German assault in 1918 and over 14,6000 names are inscribed here. Henry John Sims was entitled to the British Medal and the Victory Medal.

Another young soldier whose name is not commemorated anywhere in Alderbury, was killed during the MICHAEL Offensive three days later. He was Private Archibald (Archie) Burt of Salisbury.

ARCHIBALD FRANK BURT
33305 Private
1st Battalion The Wiltshire Regiment
Died 24 March 1918. Aged 20

He spent his boyhood in Alderbury and was a pupil of Alderbury School. His parents, Henry and Emma Jane Burt, moved to Ashfield Road, Salisbury and Archie is named on the Salisbury Memorial. He was in the 1st Battalion of the Wiltshire Regiment, part of the 25th Division of Byng's Third Army deployed to the north of the Fifth Army. The battalion was in reserve and later on the first day came into action at Fremicourt, east of Bapaume. Archie died on 24 March and is named on the Arras Memorial to the Missing. He won the British War Medal and the Victory Medal.

During the first few days of the MICHAEL Offensive the Germans recaptured all the land they had lost on the Somme in the previous two years, including the town of Albert. It is thought that Alderbury's Reynold Rolls of the 6th Wiltshires was taken prisoner during this time.

REYNOLD GEORGE ROLLS
9288 Private
6th Battalion The Wiltshire Yeomanry
Prisoner of war
Died in captivity 7 November 1918. Aged 24.

Reynold Rolls was the younger brother of Hedley Rolls who died in Mesopotamia a month later. His parents, George and Elizabeth Rolls and his brothers and sisters lived on Vicarage Lane, Alderbury. Reynold enlisted in Devizes on 13 August 1914. He was attached to the 2nd Wiltshires before transferring to the 6th. From 1915 onwards he served in France and Flanders until taken prisoner. He died in captivity in Germany just days before the armistice. It has not been possible to find details of his internment as German prisoner-of-war records from WWI for non-officers were destroyed in a bombing raid on Berlin in 1945. A clue to the probable date of his capture is to be found in an item in the Salisbury Times of 3 May 1918. It quotes from the Alderbury Parish Paper and includes the following words:

> The great battle that has been going on intermittently since March 21st has taken toll of Alderbury men. Victor Eyres, Victor England and Reynold Rolls are prisoners.[15]

From the beginning of 1918, the 6th Wiltshires had had a fairly quiet time with few casualties and none reported missing. At the beginning of March, the battalion moved from trenches near the Hindenburg Line to the third line of defence around Doignies and Morchies villages, halfway between Cambrai and Bapaume. Here they worked on defences and trained with mortars. When the MICHAEL Offensive was launched in the early morning mist of 21 March and during the following day, the 6th Wiltshire moved along the line supporting the brigades in front of them and ready for a counter-attack. When its position, too, came under attack, the enemy was checked with rifle-fire and Lewis guns. During that night the troops ahead began to fall back and the third-line defence then became the first line of resistance. Patrols went out early the next morning and found much of the area in enemy hands, Morchies captured and their right flank unprotected, making movement difficult. The position again came under heavy fire from a considerable force and despite stubborn resistance it became enveloped. Withdrawal proved impossible and it was decided to try to hold on until nightfall. By 5pm there was no option but to retreat to the next system of defence. Many men sacrificed their lives in providing cover for their comrades as they withdrew under a heavy barrage and severe crossfire from machine guns. On re-forming at 6pm they could muster only 38 from more than 480 men. Shelling continued through the next night and the next day, but, reinforced by a new draft of 64 men, the remnants eventually reached Baupaume. There the 6th Wiltshires fought in the battles of Bapaume and Grevilliers, a rearguard action from unfavourable ground. Again they fought stubbornly but suffered heavily. Only an officer and 18 other ranks were left. The action of the 6th Wiltshires was described in a report by Commanding Officers as: *an heroic episode of self-sacrifice stemming the victorious rush of a superior enemy and a model lesson of rearguard fighting.*[15]

It seems likely that sometime during this battle Pte Reynold Rolls was captured and then interned. He died in Germany a few days before the Armistice. He is buried at Cologne Southern Cemetery, Germany. V.H.3. The cemetery was used during the war for the burial of more than one thousand Allied prisoners and after the war was chosen as one of four permanent cemeteries to which British graves from 183 cemeteries in Germany were moved. Pte Reynold Rolls was awarded the 1914-15 Star, the British War Medal and the Victory Medal.

THE GEORGETTE OFFENSIVE: 9 APRIL 1918

On 9 April 1918, the Germans launched another great offensive, code-named GEORGETTE. This was an attempt to capture the Channel ports and drive the BEF back into the sea. It was first directed against a new and inexperienced Portugese division that was soon overpowered and driven back to the River Lys. This was followed by an attack by two armies north and south of the town of Armentières. This succeeded in pushing the BEF back for 10 miles, almost to the brink of defeat. Field Marshall Haig issued an urgent directive to his troops:

> *There is no other course open to us but to fight it out. Every position must be held to the last man: there must be no retirement. With our backs to the wall and believing in the justice of our cause, each one must fight to the end.*

On 21 April the 1st Battalion of the Hampshire Regiment, with 19 year-old Pte Robert Bundy, encamped near a wood to the north of Bethune and south of Armentières.

ROBERT HENRY BUNDY
43330 Private
1st Battalion The Hampshire Regiment
Died 22 April 1918. Aged 19.

Robert Henry was the son of Robert and Ellen Bundy of Littleton, Junction Road, Alderbury. He was born and brought up in the village. In the 1901 census Robert, then aged two, was residing with his parents, his brother Thomas (who lost his life at Somme in 1916) and his sister Vera. He enlisted in Salisbury and was attached to the 1st Hampshire Battalion.

The Hampshire Regiment History (Vol.2) describes the battle that took place on Monday 22 April 1918, the day that Robert Bundy was killed. The 1st Hampshires were involved in the Battle of Bethune and its objective was to attack Pacault Wood, a few kilometres north of the town and across a canal opposite Gonnehem. The wood was occupied by the enemy, giving them cover and a tactical advantage in the event of a mass offensive. A surprise attack was planned under cover of early morning darkness and at dawn three companies were in position, with a fourth

Pacult Wood near Bethune

company in support on the southern bank of the canal. A heavy trench mortar barrage was put down on the southern edge of the wood. Then the canal had to be crossed by footbridges thrown over by the Royal Engineers. Immediately these became the scene of many casualties from answering fire. The companies advanced by platoons along the edge and inside the thick wood using the paths. The battle raged all day and into the evening, There was continuous attack and counter-attack within the wood itself and along the canal bank with the constant noise of bursting shells, machine gun fire and the peppering of rifle shots. A

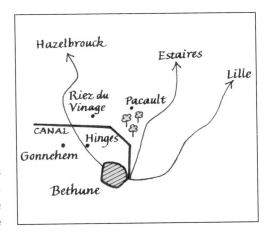

soldier who took part in the attack described the scene in a letter to his parents published in the Hampshire Chronicle a few months later. He wrote:

> ...Then all at once we heard them talking; we were within 20 or 30 yards of them before they saw us or we them. They were chattering away like as if they were making plans, but directly they saw us they put their machine guns on us and we opened fire on them. ...we were subjected to one of the heaviest bombardments ever known. When we went into the wood there was scarcely a shellhole but, when we had finished, it was simply blown to pieces. [16]

The Battle of Pacault Wood was a victory for the 1st Hampshire with the ground won, 70 prisoners taken and weaponry gained. Losses were heavy with five officers and 43 other ranks killed or missing. Pte Robert Bundy was one of those killed in action that day. His name is engraved on panel 73 of the Loos Memorial Wall, in Pas de Calais, which commemorates over 20,000 men who have no known grave. He was awarded the British War Medal and the Victory Medal.

In late spring or early summer, Private Maurice Kerly of the 7th Somersets was captured and taken prisoner.

MAURICE ADOLPHUS KERLY
38712 Private
7th Battalion, The Somerset Light Infantry
Prisoner of war
Died in captivity of wounds. Aged 19.
*assumed date of death 3 May 1918 in France
(as stated on British Military Death Certificate)
Actual date of death 6 July 1918
(recorded on Red Cross Certificate relating to German authority) [17]

*The assumed date of death is almost certainly the date when Maurice was last with his army unit and possibly when, perhaps wounded, he became a prisoner of war. POW records of non-officers in WWI were destroyed in a bombing raid on Berlin in 1945.

Maurice was born on 5 February 1899 at Barford St Martin, the son of Walter and Ellen Kerly. It is assumed that he attended the local village school opposite the Kerly family house where the family lived for several years before moving to 1 Belmont Cottages, Clarendon. His father was a gardener at Belmont House and also ran a small haulage business using horse and cart. His family eagerly awaited Maurice's return when the war was over, but it was not to be. Maurice's younger brother, Harold, served with the 1st Oxfordshire and Buckinghamshire Light Infantry and survived the war. He married Bessie Trusler who was in domestic service at Kennel Farm across the road from Belmont cottages. A younger sister Florence (Lampard) went to Alderbury school and her memories are recorded in Alderbury Millennium book.[18] Maurice enlisted in the army in Salisbury and his family believe that he advanced his age. His medal card indicates that he served overseas after 1 January 1916. It may be assumed that the 19 year-old Maurice Kerly was taken prisoner on or around 3 May 1918, the date that he was known to be missing, presumed dead. He died of wounds while in internment in Germany on 6 July 1918. While captive, Maurice sent a postcard written in pencil to his parents at Belmont Cottages, Alderbury.

It says:

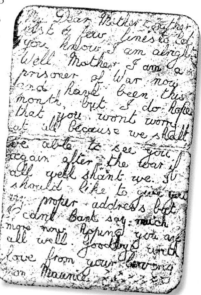

My Dear Mother and Father
Just a few lines to let you know I am alright. Well
Mother I am a prisoner of War now and have been
this month, but I do hope that you wont worry at
all because we shall be able to see you again
after the war if all well shant we. I should like to
give you a proper address but I cant. Cant say
much more now hoping you are all well.
Goodbye with love from your loving son
Maurice xxxxx

Maurice did not return home. His card, postmarked 30 June 1918, reveals that he had been a prisoner for about a month, although it is not exactly known how or when he was captured or the nature of his wounds. His battalion, the 7th Somersets in the 20th Division, served in France and Flanders. The 20th Division had been in the thick of the fighting from July 1915 when it first arrived in France. In the German spring offensives of 1918 it had suffered badly with many losses. On 20 April, after heavy fighting in the old Somme battlefields, the whole Division was withdrawn to an area south west of Amiens to await reinforcements. It was sometime after this that Maurice was captured.

Pte Maurice Kerly was interned at Fest.Las.1 Strasbourg. He is buried in the Allied Plot, Row 3 Grave 121, Cronenbourg, French National Cemetery, Strasbourg. His name is also commemorated in the Parish Church of Barford St Martin, near Salisbury and in the Golden Book of Remembrance at Wells Cathedral, Somerset. He was awarded the British War Medal and the Victory Medal.

copy of his postcard

FRANCE: THE FINAL MONTHS

There is no doubt that in the spring and early summer of 1918 the German advances were spectacular as Allied positions were overrun and ground that had been won at so much cost earlier in the war, was retaken. Yet, each time, on the brink of victory, the enemy offensives lost momentum as supply lines failed to keep up with exhausted and ravenously hungry troops. Each offensive ground to a halt without achieving its main objective – that of dividing and defeating the British and the French armies.

The first days of August 1918 saw the beginning of 100 days of Allied successes that brought the Great War to an end that November. The first of the victories, the Battle of Amiens, began at 4.20am on the 8 August in heavy mist. Its objective was to clear the railroad between Amiens and Paris in order to relieve the pressure on the vital communication centre at Amiens. It was fought by the Allied Fourth Army of Canadians and Australians, supported by 11 British divisions, alongside the French First Army. Pte Leslie Northeast of the 1st Dorsets, of the 32nd Division, lost his life in the Battle of Amiens.

LESLIE LEONARD NORTHEAST
34291 Private
1st Battalion, The Dorsetshire Regiment
14th Brigade, 32nd Division
Died 11 August 1918. Aged 26.

Leslie Northeast was the son of Charles George and Agnes Northeast and brother of Victor, who served on the Home Front. The family lived in one of a terrace of three cottages named Mount Pleasant, Folly Lane, Alderbury, now demolished. Leslie enlisted in Devizes although the date is not known.

The 32nd Division, including the 1st Dorsets, was held in GHQ reserve for the first two days of the battle and then passed under Canadian Corps Command attacking the Amiens to Roye road on the 9 August 1918. The Dorsetshire Regimental History relates that on the night of 10 August they bivouacked near Le Quesnoy in front of the enemy-held village of Damery, two miles from the town of Roye, awaiting orders. These arrived early on the morning of the 11th, but subsequently they proved to be based on confused and inaccurate intelligence. It was to be a two-battalion attack. The 1st Dorsets were ordered to capture and hold the village of Damery and Damery Wood in conjunction with the 5/6th Royal Scots taking the village of Parvillers to their left. A dawn attack was out of the question because supporting tanks could not be assembled in time. So, from the moment the men left their starting trenches at 9.30am in bright light, they were clearly visible to the enemy and subjected to intense, targeted machine gun fire. A heavy barrage intended to weaken enemy artillery the night before, had overshot by 500 yards leaving German machine guns intact and easily able to stop the advance of the Royal Scots towards Parvillers.

All four Dorset companies were positioned in old British trenches across an expanse of 2,000 yards and they infiltrated right and left to get as near as possible to their objectives. As the men went over the top at zero hour they met concentrated and deadly shellfire from the direction of Parvillers and it was a miracle that the whole battalion was not decimated. An anti-tank gun concealed in the cornfield disabled six of the eight supporting tanks. Fierce fighting and shelling went on in and around the fields and woods all day. The enemy was forced to evacuate Damery Wood but by nightfall platoons of the 1st Dorsets were pinned down on the outskirts of Damery Village.

It is not known to which company Pte Leslie Northeast was attached, but on that day there were 14 officers killed or wounded, 24 other ranks killed and 240 wounded, and 42 men were missing. Damery Village was eventually captured a few days later by Canadian troops who relieved the battalion that night. Pte Leslie Northeast is buried at Bouchoir New British Cemetery, Somme. There are over 750 war casualties commemorated on this site. They include the graves of 37 soldiers brought from the British cemetery at Damery almost all of whom belonged to 1st Dorsets or 5/6th Royal Scots. Leslie Northeast was awarded the British War Medal and the Victory Medal.

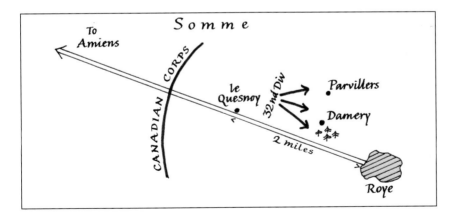

Damery and Parvillers, Battle of Amiens August 1918

CHAPTER 8

WAR CASUALTIES SENT HOME

The crossed rifles on his sleeves were awarded for marksmanship skills and the 5-star star is related to accuracy between 200 and 800 yards.

HARRY MUSSELWHITE
4975 Company Sergeant Major
6th (Service) Battalion The Wiltshire Regiment
Died of wounds 29 April 1918. Aged 38.

Harry was born in Hanging Langford, Wiltshire, son of agricultural labourer James Musselwhite and his wife, Emma. He had three brothers and a sister. In 1898, aged 18 and employed as a carter, he enlisted as a regular soldier with the 1st Battalion The Wiltshire Regiment and he served in India until 1909 and then in South Africa until 1913. He married his wife, Lena Bailey, on Christmas Eve, 1913 at Devizes after 12 years of courtship. Soon after the start of the Great War he joined the 6th Wiltshires. As an experienced soldier and expert marksman he would have been invaluable for training new recruits. He seemed to be a lover of poetry for he sometimes enclosed his own romantic and patriotic compositions in his letters to his wife. By 1917 he was in action in France where the 6th Battalion was located on the French/Belgian border and at Ypres. Harry is thought to have been wounded in the leg, although there is no record of when or how this happened. The wound became gangrenous and he was sent back to hospital in England for treatment. He died several months later on 29 April 1918. He was awarded the British War Medal and the Victory Medal.

His wife Lena lived at Walden Cottage, West Grimstead. For many years she looked after her brother-in-law Will Elliot, a forester, who suffered shell shock from his time at

Ypres; his wife, her sister Eva who was disabled; and a young niece, the daughter of another sister who had died. Lena herself died in 1972.

Harry Musselwhite is buried near the northwest corner of Alderbury Church Cemetery, plot 441. A white cross marks his grave. His name is on the Great War Plaque inside the church but not among the names of those 'At Rest', even though he died six months before the war ended. Strangely, it is among those who served overseas and survived.

When I think of you, the shadow
That surround the lonely day
Seem to fold their wings of darkness
And in the silence pass away.
All the hours are filled with music
Like the echo of your voice
The remembrance that you love me
Makes this heart of mine rejoice.
I am proud that I have found you
I am glad to know you true
Sorrow dies and sadness passes
When I think of you

When I think of you, my spirit
And my heart unite in prayer
For I thank the fate that sent you
To make life to me more fair.
There is hope where once was longing
There is rest where once was strife
Something greater, deeper, nobler
In the daily toil of life
For the knowledge that you love me
Dwells in everything I do
Though apart we are not parted
When I think of you.

Poem from C/Sgt.-Major Harry Musselwhite's notebook circa 1916

Demobilisation and the return of soldiers to their families in Great Britain from the many theatres of war was a slow process. Pte Edward Earney was in India at the time of the Armistice. He had been away for a long time and was suffering from illness. He arrived back to Chowringhee House Lodge, Clarendon, late in February 1919. Sadly, he had little time to enjoy the reunion with his family.

EDWARD THOMAS EARNEY
202999 Private
1st/4th Battalion The Dorsetshire Regiment
Died 2 March 1919 in Salisbury Infirmary. Aged 24.

Edward was the second son of William James and Phoebe Earney of Alderbury. He had a brother Victor, who also served in the Middle East, and a sister Olive. The family lived at the lodge of Chowringhee House (now known as Alderbury Hill House) on Southampton Road. The owners, the Osmond family, employed his father and one of his tasks was to operate the pump that supplied water from a deep well to the big house – a time consuming exercise.

According to a Salisbury Times Obituary report of March 28th, 1918, Edward Earney served with his battalion for four and a half years. He went to India in October 1914, served for two years in Mesopotamia and was then sent back to India. After an illness he returned to England and was declared medically unfit. He was demobilised on 21 February 1919. Immediately after his return home, on the first day of March, he was taken ill again and admitted to Salisbury Infirmary where he died the next day of double pneumonia.

He is buried in St Mary's Churchyard, Alderbury. His grave has a Commonwealth War Graves Commission headstone. He was awarded 1914 - 15 Star, the British War Medal and the Victory Medal.

SURVIVORS OF THE GREAT WAR NAMED ON ST MARY'S CHURCH PLAQUE

On Service Overseas

Capt. Albert Angel R.Fusiliers. MC
Cpl. Robert Bailey R.E.
Gnr. Charles Barber R.G.A
Pte. Frederick Bartlam R.A.S.C
Q.M.S Frederick Brewer Canadian.Rlwy Troop
Pte. Jesse Brewer Canadian Highlanders
L/c Walter Brewer R.F.C
Gnr. William Bundy Canadian. M.G.C
Str. Abraham Belstone H.M.S Kent
Pte. Leonard Bowden Labour Corps
Sgt. Alan Carse R.E.
Sgt Albert Coole R.M.A
Sgt Harry Cox R.A.V.C. MSM
Pte. George Cox Wilts. Reg.
Pte. Charles Dean R.A.S.C
Pte. Ernest Dicks M.G.C
Pte. Josiah Dowding Manchester Reg.
Pte. Frederick Dowty Essex Reg.
Pte. Edwin Dowty Wilts. Reg.
Lieut. Albert Dowty R.A.S.C.
Pte. Edwin G. Dowty. R.Irish Reg.
Pte. Victor Earney Wilts. Reg.
L/c A.C. Harry England R.F.C
Pte. Ronald England Wilts. Reg.
Sgt. Victor England Grenadier Guards
Pte. Victor Eyres Wilts Reg.
Pte. Percy Fry R.A.S.C
Pte. Gilbert Fry R.M.L.I
Str. Frederick Gambling R.N
Pte. Stanley Gray R.A.S.C
Pte. Howard Gray D.C.L.I
Pte. Ralph Gray Devon Reg.
Cpl. Charles Gulliver Wilts Reg.
Gnr. Albert Hallett R.F.A
Pte. Claude Hatcher Wilts Reg.
Sgt. Maurice Hatcher R.G.A

L/c. Percy Hatcher Middlesex Reg.
Cpl. Sidney Hatcher D.C.L.I
L/c William Hatcher Wilts Reg.
Bomr. Edward Hatcher R.G.A
Pte. Frank Harris Wilts Reg.
Dr. Jesse Hickman Canadian. F.A
P.O Thomas Hazel HMS Venus
Pte. James Hutchings R.M.L.I
Sgt. Harry Ingram Hants Reg.
Pte. Charles Kemp Wilts Reg.
Pte. Clarence Lander Wilts Reg.
Pte. Bertram Lever R.M.L.I
Pte. Harry Lock R.B.
Gnr. William Mason R.F.A
Sgt. Reginald Mouland Wilts Reg.
Sgt. Ralph Mouland R.F.A
Sgt Wilfred Moody R.A.S.C
Sgt. Algernon Maidment R.E
Staff Sgt. Hedley Maidment R.A.S.C
Gnr. Cyril Maidment R.F.A
Pte. Felton Maidment R.M.L.I
Pte. Cecil Newman Labour Corps
Pte. Thomas Northeast R.West Kent Reg.
Pte. Frederick Northeast R.A.M.C
Pte. James Northeast Canadian.Labour Corps
L/c William Newell Hants Reg.
Lieut. Percival Osmond Hants Reg.
Pte. Frederick Prewett Wilts. Reg.
Pte. William Prewett R.Warwick Reg.
Sgt. Ethelbert Parfitt Wilts Reg.
Pte. Thomas Rumbold Welsh Fus. M.M.
Driver William Rolls R.F.A
Pte. Stanley Richardson W.Riding Reg.
Driver William Richardson R.G.A
Bomr. Reginald Russell R.G.A
Pte. William Russell R.G.A
Pte. Alfred Shorter Hants Reg.

Pte. Percy Shorter R.A.S.C
Pte. Herbert Sims Hants Reg.
Pte. Frank Thomas R. Wilts Yeo
Sgt. Charles Tucker Canadian. Inf.
Cpl. Charles Vincent R.A.S.C
AB William Vincent R.N
Cpl. Henry Willis Welsh Guards
Sgt Frederick Willis Wilts Reg.
Pte. William Willis R.M.L.I
Gnr. Walter White R.F.A

On Home Service

Pte. Samuel Bundy R.Berks Reg.
Q.M.S. Henry Cox Wilts Reg.
Pte. John Cox Labour Corps
Gnr. Ernest Crook R.F.A
Cpl. William Dean Devon Reg.
Pte. George Dicks Wilts Reg.
Pte. Victor Hawtin R.A.S.C
C.S.M. William Hyman Labour
   Corps
C.F. Thomas Jervis R.A.C.D.
Pte. Victor Northeast R.A.V.C.
Pte. Alfred Rolls Devon Reg.
Pte. Harry Russell Wilts Reg.
Pte. Charles Sheppard Devon Reg.
Pte. Walter Tanner Devon Reg.
Pte. Lionel Whitcher R.A.S.C

Abbreviations

R.E. Royal Engineers
R.G.A. Royal Garrison Artillery
R.A.S.C. Royal Army Service Corps
R.F.C. Royal Flying Corps
R.M.A. Royal Marines Artillery
R.M.L.I. Royal Marines Light
   Infantry
R.F.A. Royal Field Artillery
R.N. Royal Navy
R.B. Rifle Brigade
R.A.M.C. Royal Army Medical
   Corps
R.A.V.C. Royal Army Veterinary
   Corps
R.A.C.D. Royal Army Chaplains
   Dept
D.C.L.I. Duke of Cornwall's Light
   Infantry
F.A. Field Ambulance
MGC Machine Gun Corps
M.C. Military Cross
M.M. Military Medal
M.S.M. Meritorious Service Medal

GALLANTRY MEDALS OF SURVIVORS

THE MILITARY CROSS
Second-Lieutenant Albert Angel, Royal Fusiliers

Albert was born in Downton in 1881, the fifth son of the thirteen children of John Angel, farm labourer and his wife, Nelly. He was one of the first pupils of Bishop Wordsworth School and lived in Whiteparish at the time. He lodged during the week with his eldest sister in St Martin's Church Street, Salisbury, walking home on Fridays and back on Mondays. From 1921 to 1931, Captain Albert Angel and his wife lived at Oaklands, Clarendon Road and he was a County Court bailiff at Salisbury. He had a distinguished army record in the South African War and the Younghusband Expedition to Tibet in 1904. His son likens his build and some of his mannerisms to that of Captain Mainwaring of 'Dad's Army'. An older brother lived next to the old Primitive Methodist Chapel in Whaddon.

> *Citation*
>
> *Assisted by only one man, under very heavy shell-fire, he dug out three very deeply buried men and while doing this he was twice knocked down by shell-fire. He kept full control of his platoon in very trying circumstances. He has done consistently good work throughout the campaign.* [19]

THE MILITARY MEDAL
1918. Private Tom Rumbold, Royal Welsh Fusiliers

Tom was transferred to the Welsh Fusiliers from the Army Service Corps in 1916 and went to France in 1917. After a series of engagements he won the Military Medal, with others of his company, just before the GEORGETTE attack on Kemmel Hill, near Ypres, in April 1918. Tom Rumbold came from an old Alderbury family. He lived at Totterdown Cottage on Folly Lane and is listed in Brown's Trade Directory of 1925 as a carpenter. He married the Countess of Radnor's maid and died in 1959 at the age of 77.

> *Citation*
>
> *His Majesty the King has been graciously pleased to approve the award of the Military Medal for bravery in the field to the undermentioned…….60401 Private T. Rumbold* [20]

THE MERITORIOUS SERVICE MEDAL
Sergeant Harry Cox, Royal Army Veterinary Corps

Sgt Harry Cox RAVC was awarded the Meritorious Service Medal that after 1916 was awarded for an act of meritorious service or gallantry behind the lines, i.e. not in the face of the enemy. We have been unable to find the citation in the London Gazette. He lived with his wife in the caretaker's cottage next to the old Reading Room on The Green, both buildings are now demolished.

NOTES

1   www.hmshampshire.co.uk A minute by minute account of Hampshire's last voyage; a list of the men lost; newspaper reports and speculation, frauds and conspiracy theories.

2   Page 213: Nicholson, GWL. (1962) Canadian Expeditionary Force 1914 – 1919. Official History of the Canadian Army in the First World War. Queen's Printer,Ottawa

3   ibid pp 147-154

4   Salisbury Times: In Memoriam column; 22 July 1921

5   Brown's Trade Directory 1925

6   1881 census, Alton, Hampshire

7   Nicholson, GWL supra pp167-174

8   5th Btn Diary Wiltshire Regiment June 1915 – Feb 1919: R.G.B.W Wardrobe Museum Trust 2002 - www.thewardrobe.com

9   Jerrold, Douglas: (1923) The Royal Naval Division. Hutchinson & co.

10 ibid page 211.

11 Page, Christopher (1999). Command in the Royal Naval Division. A Military Biography of Brig. Gen. AM Asquith Spellmount Staplehurst, Kent.

12 Nicholson, GWL: supra pp 247 – 258

13 ibid: pp 279 – 281

14 Jerrold, Douglas (1925) pp 179-181 The Hawke Battalion. Ernest Benn Ltd

15 Salisbury Times 3 May 1918

16 Hampshire Chronicle 31 Aug 1918

17 Information provided by the family from Sunset Militaria, Dinedor Cross, Herefordshire,HR2 6PF; Index of Army War Deaths 1914 – 1921; Family Records Centre, London; International Red Cross Tracing Agency, Geneva, Switzerland Embassy of the Federal Republic of Germany, London

18 AWLHRG (2000) Alderbury & Whaddon - A Millennium Mosaic of People, Places and Progress.

19 Citation: Salisbury Times 3 Nov 1916

20 Citation: London Gazette 10 Sept 1918

Please note that the web-sites were accessed in May 2004

WORLD WAR II

Went the day well?
We died and never knew
But, well or ill,
Freedom, we died for you.

Anon

by

BERNICE RANGE

INTRODUCTION

In 1947 the people of Alderbury and Whaddon paid tribute to the men and women from the area who had served in the Armed Forces during World War II. A party to celebrate their safe return also served as a remembrance for those who lost their lives in defence of the freedom we know today. Of the men who lost their lives, 14 are named on the War Memorial standing on The Green and 12 on the Memorial in St Mary's Church. Some are named on both memorials and others are not named but may be buried in the churchyard or elsewhere.

This section traces the lives of these young men and looks at the progress of the war in the various Theatres of Operations where they fought and died. The many other brave men and women who served in the conflict and returned home safely are remembered in the final chapter.

In January 1933 Adolf Hitler became Chancellor of Germany and began a programme of re-armament. World War II began when the German Army invaded Poland on 1 September 1939, twenty one years after the end of World War I, which had been called *the war to end all wars*. By the evening of 3 September, Britain and France, who were committed by treaty to help Poland, were at war with Germany. Within a week, Australia, New Zealand, Canada and South Africa had also joined the conflict. The war in Europe aided Japanese expansionism in the Far East and the Tripartite Pact between Germany, Italy and Japan was signed in September 1940. The conflict became global when America joined the Allies after the attack on Pearl Harbour in December 1941.

World War II lasted for six long and bloody years and was eventually to involve every major world power and cost the lives of 60 million people, civilians as well as military personnel. For most people living during those years the progress of the war and the complex nature of events were shrouded in ignorance and propaganda. Governments controlled the level and content of information available to the general public and today, many people view those years through the glamorised eyes of the Hollywood movie.

The War in Europe ended with the German surrender in May 1945 when the Allied Armies advancing from the west, met the Soviet Armies advancing from the east. Japan surrendered on 29 August 1945 after the Allies wiped out the cities of Hiroshima and Nagasaki with Atomic bombs. No engine of warfare had ever possessed such power and the world shuddered.............. So victory came.

CHAPTER 9

EUROPE 1939 – 40

In September 1939 Britain and all the Commonwealth countries, together with France and Poland, were at war with Germany and an Army was quickly raised and sent to France. This army was called the British Expeditionary Force (BEF) and concentrated on fortifying a sector of the front along the Belgian border. In May 1940 when Germany invaded The Netherlands and Belgium, the BEF advanced to meet the attack. The German Army adopted the weapon of Blitzkrieg, a new strategy for deep fast penetration with air support which left the static positions of the Belgian and Anglo French Armies vulnerable. The use of armoured columns supported by dive-bombers and motorised infantry on narrow fronts pierced the Allied defences in several places. German forces crossed the River Meuse at Sedan on 13 May and reached the Channel coast at Abbeville on 20 May, severing the BEF from its bases in Normandy and cutting the Allied front in half. This armoured thrust opened a sixty mile wide corridor behind the back of the Allied left wing in Belgium.

Unsuccessful counter attacks on German Panzer forces on 21 May by General Gort at Arras and by General de Gaulle at Montcornet did however slow the advance. From Abbeville, the German tanks turned north and captured Boulogne and Calais. On 26 May the BEF was ordered

Battle of
Flanders

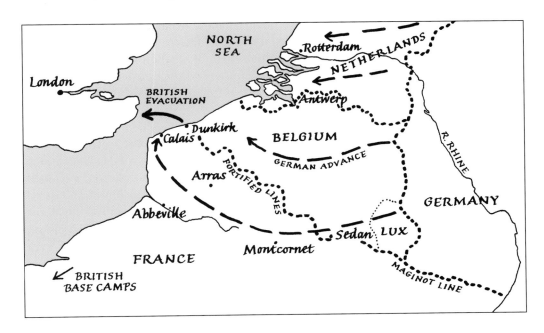

to withdraw to the coast for evacuation. The following day the exhausted Belgian Army on the left flank was compelled to surrender and, in a series of hard fought actions, the BEF and part of the French First Army withdrew to the coastal area. This withdrawal was helped by a valiant stand by that part of the French First Army which was cut off near Lille.

THE EVACUATION OF DUNKIRK

The evacuation of the trapped BEF from France, after the German break-through began on 26 May 1940. The operation, which was codenamed DYNAMO, was organised and controlled by Vice Admiral Ramsey, Commander of Dover. Over a calm sea a fleet of 900 boats of all sizes from destroyers to privately owned pleasure craft ferried in the region of 338,000 troops from inlets, jetties and beaches around Dunkirk, the main harbours having been destroyed by bombing. The initial defensive perimeter ran from Dunkirk to Nieuport along the Aa, Scarpe, and Yser canal line but contracted daily. Rearguard actions by units of the BEF maintained this defensive perimeter until 4 June.

The German army did not send forward their tank divisions which could have easily cut through the line but relied on Luftwaffe attack on the beleaguered troops on the beaches. It has since been reported that Hermann Goring, the Commander-in-Chief of the Luftwaffe, for reasons of prestige and political purpose persuaded Hitler that the job could be better accomplished by air power. Many troops waiting for evacuation from the beaches were killed in these air attacks but the RAF was able to inflict damage on the German airforce. The major tragedy of the evacuation was the sinking of the Cunard liner *Lancastria*, which was evacuating troops, with the loss of 3,000 lives.

Several Alderbury and Whaddon men who were killed in later campaigns were successfully evacuated from the beaches at Dunkirk. Colonel Samuel Alexander Holwell Kirkby (then acting Lt. Col) of the Royal Sussex regiment was in charge of Lines of Communication and was one of the last to leave the beaches arriving at Falmouth on 18 June 1940. Driver Edward George Grout was safely evacuated from the beaches only to die later in the Far East.

Lance Sergeant Frederick William Carter of the 17th Field Company (Coy) Royal Engineers who was killed on 1 June 1940 during the evacuation from Dunkirk is commemorated on Column 21 of the Dunkirk Memorial as having died at sea with no known grave.

FREDERICK WILLIAM CARTER
1866709 Lance Sergeant
17th Field Coy Royal Engineers
Died 1 June 1940. Aged 28.

Frederick William Carter was born in Peterborough on 13 November 1911 and enlisted into the Royal Engineers (RE) as a Boy Soldier in August 1927 at the age of 15 years. His parents, George and Florence lived in Barnsley but at the time of his death in 1940 his mother was living on Clarendon Road in Alderbury. As an Army Apprentice Tradesman he qualified as a mason at the age of 18 years. He was then promoted to Sapper and in November 1931 he was posted to 2nd Field Coy RE serving in Egypt. Since the abolition of the British Protectorate over Egypt in 1922, Britain had kept a garrison there to protect the Suez Canal and train the Egyptian Army. Frederick Carter as a member of the RE was involved with the strengthening of defences and improving communications within the Suez Canal Zone.

In 1939 he returned to Britain and was promoted to Corporal. On 19th September he left for France with the 17th Coy RE, a mechanised unit forming part of the 3rd Division, BEF. He was promoted to Lance Sgt in February 1940 and at the retreat to Dunkirk his division was on the left flank of the BEF. Royal Engineer units were involved in blowing up bridges and roads to slow the enemy advance. Frederick Carter was killed on 1 June 1940 during the withdrawal and is commemorated on the Dunkirk Memorial as:

presumed to be drowned while being evacuated from Dunkirk.

He was awarded the War Medal 1939-45 and the 1939-45 Star. He is commemorated on the Alderbury War Memorial and on the church memorial.

THE DUNKIRK MEMORIAL

The Dunkirk Memorial is situated in Dunkirk Town Cemetery and commemorates 4,534 soldiers of the BEF who died during the evacuation from Dunkirk and who have no known grave. The cemetery also contains 810 Commonwealth war graves. The Memorial was designed by Philip Hepworth and the engraved glass panel depicting the evacuation was designed by John Hutton who also designed the Great West Screen in the rebuilt Coventry Cathedral.

After Dunkirk there was a real threat of invasion for Britain. The German Army had 3,000 barges capable of holding 500,000 men waiting to cross the English Channel once they achieved air superiority. The south coast of England was fortified and the Home Guard put on alert. Although many troops had been evacuated safely from France, the Army was severely weakened by the loss of arms and equipment. The Prime Minister, Winston Churchill, rallied the nation with his famous speech, which included the passage:

> ....*We shall defend our Island, whatever the cost may be, we shall fight on the beaches, we shall fight on the landing grounds, we shall fight in the fields and in the streets, we shall fight in the hills; we shall never surrender.......*

CHAPTER 10

THE FAR EAST

1941: THE FALL OF HONG KONG

Prior to the outbreak of World War II the British Crown Colony of Hong Kong, in its strategically important location off the south coast of China, was headquarters to the Royal Navy China Squadron. The channel between the north coast of Hong Kong Island and the mainland formed a magnificent harbour and the whole area had been ceded to Britain in 1842. China had been at war with Japan since 1937, resisting incursions into its territories. She officially joined the Allies on 9 December 1941 when the Imperial Japanese Army began its East Asia Campaign. The British Military were unprepared for the speed of the Japanese attacks in the Far East and the Colony was an early victim of the Campaign launched at the same time as the attack on the American naval base at Pearl Harbour.

Hong Kong area

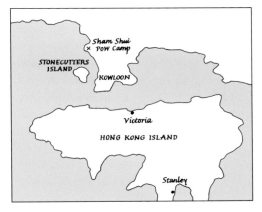

On 8 December 1941 the Japanese 38th Division struck at the British line on the mainland. The line was defended by a small garrison consisting of British, Indian and Canadian troops under the command of Brigadier Wallis. At the same time, Japanese aircraft attacked the RAF base at Kai Tak Airfield, destroying or immobilising the aircraft there. British resistance depended on holding the Gin Drinkers Line, the one weakly prepared defensive line that stretched across the Kowloon Peninsular. However, their positions were heavily raided from the air and under constant ground attack. C Company Punjabis and Royal Engineers started a delaying rearguard action, blowing up bridges and tunnels in front of the advancing Japanese. The key strong point on the line, the Shing Mun Redoubt, was expected to be held for at least a week but it was merely a few pillboxes joined by tunnels and surrounded by wire and fell quickly to the attack. The ferocity of the Japanese attacks and the heavy casualties sustained, forced General Maltby to withdraw the troops from the mainland to Hong Kong Island for the final defence of the Colony.

The withdrawal was completed by 13 December and the forces were reorganised for the defence of Hong Kong Island. The north shore of the island was heavily shelled from the mainland and the Japanese request for a formal surrender was refused. Hong Kong Island was invaded on 18 December and heavy fighting ensued through the mountainous terrain, which comprises most of the island. The coastal approach to the capital, Victoria, was heavily defended so the Japanese had struck inland to descend on it from the mountains.

The British Governor Mark Young, after consultation with General Maltby was forced to surrender the island to the Japanese on 25 December 1941. More than 11,000 men were taken as Prisoners of War (POW) including Walter Norman Wathen from Alderbury

WALTER NORMAN WATHEN
2314610 Lance Sergeant
Royal Corps of Signals
Died 1 October 1942. Aged 35.

Walter Norman Wathen was part of a large family, having six brothers and one sister, Louisa. He was the son of Tom and Emily Wathen of Exeter and husband of Kate Alice Wathen of Andover. One of his brothers, Tom, lived on Clarendon Road and worked for the Post Office. Walter joined the army at 14 years of age and served in the Royal Corps of Signals, attached to various units over the years. In 1942 he was serving with the Hong Kong Signals Corps. Their role when the Japanese attacked was basically that of problem fixers, going to the aid of any unit whose communication equipment had been damaged by enemy fire. He was captured by the Japanese at the fall of the Colony and his service record states that he was missing as a POW following the sinking of a ship and was posted as killed in action at sea. It is known that the Japanese Army transported large numbers of prisoners by sea to labour camps in Japan and that the vessels were unmarked cargo ships. Several were sunk by Allied firepower. It has recently been discovered through the meticulous and ongoing research of Hong Kong based historian Tony Banham that Walter was lost onboard the Japanese cargo ship *Lisbon Maru* after an attack by the American submarine *USS Grouper*.

He is commemorated at the Sai Wan Memorial, Hong Kong, column 9. This memorial honours over 2,000 men of the land forces of the British Commonwealth who died in the defence of Hong Kong and stands at the entrance to Sai Wan Bay War Cemetery outside Victoria. The names are inscribed on panels of Portland stone that occupy a commanding position 305m above sea level looking over the cemetery and across the water to mainland China.

THE LISBON MARU

The 22 year old ship the *Lisbon Maru* which arrived at Stonecutters Island off Kowloon in September 1942 had previously been used to transport Japanese migrants to the United States. On 25 September about 1,850 POWs were shipped across to her from Shamshuipo POW camp where they had been held prisoners for nine months since the fall of the Colony. The *Lisbon Maru* sailed for Japan two days later with the POWs and 780 Japanese soldiers, who were returning home, on board. When she was about 120 miles south east of Shanghai, at 7am on 1 October she was hit by a torpedo fired by the American submarine *Grouper*, causing serious damage. During the rest of that day the Japanese troops on board were taken off onto other troopships. The POWs were left imprisoned in the holds as the Japanese soldiers had battened down the hatches when they left. They remained in the holds for 26 hours, trapped and waiting to drown in appalling conditions of filth, disease, and malnutrition. As the boat began to settle they broke out from their prison and tried to swim to nearby islands but Japanese shipping in the area shot at them in the water. Soldiers from the Hong Kong Signal Corps, to which Walter Norman Wathen from Alderbury was attached, were in the upper tier of No 2 hold and lost nearly half their numbers in the sinking. Most of the men in No 2 hold made it out of the ship before it sank but were caught by currents and swept out to sea where they drowned. Eventually some of the POWs were picked up but, by the end of the day, 825 of them had died either still locked in the ship or in the water.

THE GROUPER SS 214

The United States submarine *Grouper* SS 214, was laid down at Groton, Connecticut, in 1940. She was a Gato class vessel on her second war patrol and had already sunk another Japanese freighter when she encountered the *Lisbon Maru*, off Shanghai, in October 1942. Apparently there were no signs that the ship was anything but a Japanese troop transport, so *Grouper* attacked, firing six torpedoes. Five of these Mk 14 fish either passed under the target or failed to detonate, but one exploded against the stern, bringing the *Lisbon Maru* to a standstill. The *Grouper* immediately came under attack from patrol boats and aircraft so departed the scene. The crew took one last look at the Japanese soldiers being taken off the stricken vessel and did not realise there were Allied POWs trapped in the hold. It was days later that the submarine crew picked up a radio signal stating that they had sunk a ship carrying Allied POWs. By this time the surviving POWs had been taken to Shanghai, from where they were shipped to Japan, arriving on 10 October and taken to camps at Kobe and Osaka.

1942: THE FALL OF SINGAPORE

Singapore Island is situated off the southern tip of the Malay Peninsula in Asia. The separating strip of water is crossed by a causeway and the Island which has a total area of 220 square miles was mostly low lying, swampy jungle before World War II.

The port grew up as a busy trading city after the British entrepreneur Sir Stamford Raffles leased it from the Sultan of Jahore in 1819 for the East India Company. In 1867, together with Penang and Malacca it became a colony of the British Empire. Its situation on the sea routes from Europe to Japan and China and its close proximity to the Dutch East Indies and Australia, made its commercial importance huge. Its position also made it important for Imperial defence and in 1919 Admiral Jellicoe designated it as the main base of the British Far Eastern Fleet.

The fortress was strengthened in the 1930s and became the centre of a political debate as expenditure escalated. However, the work at Changi Naval Base was finally completed in 1938. The defence of Singapore was based on potential seaborne attack and its vulnerability from an overland attack was never fully addressed. Consequently it had no defences when the Japanese attacked after they had overrun Malaya.

Singapore

On 1 February 1942 the general retreat of Allied troops from Malaya to Singapore Island over the 70ft wide causeway was completed. The Japanese by this time had control of the air and seas after a large force of dive and torpedo bombers had sunk the two British battleships, *Repulse* and *Prince of Wales* on 10 December.

The Japanese landed assault troops on the north and west parts of Singapore Island and these penetrated quickly inland. General Percival, in charge of two and a half unreinforced divisions of Allied troops was facing three divisions of crack Japanese troops under General Yamashita. As dawn broke on 15 February there was fighting in the streets on the outskirts of Singapore and by this time over one million people, mostly women and children, were trapped in a three mile radius. General Percival judged that a siege of the city of Singapore was impossible due to lack of supplies, ammunition and fresh water. At 11.30am a cease-fire was announced and Singapore was surrendered to

the Japanese at 4pm on 15 February 1942. Winston Churchill called it:
the worst disaster and largest capitulation in British history.

In the region of 132,000 Allied soldiers were taken as POWs in the battles of Malaya and Singapore. Following the surrender most of the Allied forces were held at Changi prison, on a staple diet of rice, before dispersal to labour camps.

Edward George Grout from Alderbury was one of the British soldiers taken prisoner by the Japanese in Singapore.

EDWARD GEORGE GROUT
T128549 Driver
Royal Army Service Corps
H.Q. 18th Division
Died 7 December 1943.
Aged 26.

Edward Grout age 18, taken at Odstock

Edward George Grout, or Ted as family and friends knew him, was born on 13 March 1926 in Norfolk, the son of George and Sarah Grout. His family say that as a young boy he was quite a prankster and played many naughty tricks on them but despite this he was very much loved and his mother's favourite. He had two sisters, Doris and Joan, and his younger sister Joan still remembers the way he looked after her and spoilt her. He was a self-taught carpenter and one of his friends, Peter Turner of Odstock, remembers him as being a fanatical motorcycle fan. He lived with his family in Odstock and married Edith Pearce in 1935 and had two children, Ann and Roy. His sister in law, Mrs Norris, remembers that his mother moved to Alderbury before the war and lived in a bungalow called Pennsylvania, near Lights Lane. When Ted went overseas his mother moved to Clarendon Road so that Edith and the children could live with her. She did the laundry for American troops stationed in the area as well as washing all the surplices for Alderbury church.

Ted joined the Royal Army Service Corps (RASC) as a driver on 4 December 1939. He served with various Motor Transport Companies in the UK before going to France on 4 April 1940 with the BEF. He was attached to 299 (HQ 18 Div) Coy and was amongst the final evacuees from Dunkirk leaving France on 23 June 1940, two days before the evacuation was completed. He was then on home service until October 1941 when he was posted to India. In January 1942 he left Bombay for Malaya where he fought against the Japanese and was reported missing on 15 February. The Japanese in fact took him as a POW at the fall of Singapore. He died of cerebral malaria at Kanchanaburi Hospital in Thailand while working on the notorious Burma-Siam Railway project.

The Salisbury and Winchester Journal and the Salisbury Times dated 28 May 1943 reported that his family had been notified he was safe and a POW in Japanese hands. His sister Joan says that the family all wrote regularly to him and believed that he would return but they never received a reply to any of their letters. In 1945 after the end of the war in the Far East the family received a War Office statement which told of his death in 1943.

He is remembered on the Alderbury memorials and also has a memorial in the church at Odstock where he lived before joining the army. He was awarded the War Medal 1939-45, the 1939-45 Star and the Pacific Star. He is commemorated in the Kanchanaburi War Cemetery in Thailand as one of the POWs who were forced to work on the Burma-Siam Railway.

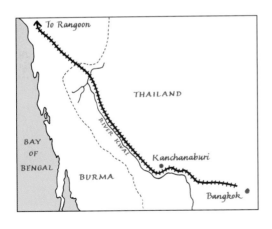

THE BURMA-SIAM RAILWAY

The building of the Burma-Siam (now Thailand) Railway was a Japanese project to improve the supply and communication line to their large army in Burma. The line started at Ban Pong, due west of Bangkok, in Thailand and ran up to the Burmese border. To build the railway the Japanese took nearly 32,000 allied POWs to work on the line, which proved to be a racial and cultural clash between western and oriental attitudes. The prisoners had to build their own camps and were divided into two forces, one at each end of the line and both working towards the centre.

On arrival at a new campsite the initial task of the POWs was to build accommodation for the Japanese guards, then the cookhouse and huts for the working parties and finally shelters for the sick. Frequently the men were sent to work on the line before their accommodation was completed. Throughout the building of the line food supplies were totally inadequate and irregular. Men frequently had to live for weeks on a small daily ration of rice flavoured with salt.

13,000 POWs died of sickness, malnutrition and exhaustion during the 14 month construction period of the 424 kilometre railway line. During the highest mortality period 700 prisoners died in six months due to a combination of monsoon conditions, hard work, poor food, cholera and dysentery. Many of those who eventually returned home were beset by ill health. Burmese and Indian labourers from the many plantations in the area were also conscripted to work on the line.

Lieutenant Usuki, Commandant Konyu 2 Camp on the Burma-Siam Railway stated:

The Japanese are prepared to work – you must work

The Japanese are prepared to eat less – you must eat less

The Japanese are prepared to die – you must be prepared to die.

It has been suggested that senior Japanese officials and commanders may not have known about conditions in different camps and perhaps did not care about the inadequate food and medical supplies. Japanese administration was exceptionally poor, there was insufficient transport when moving prisoners and marches were badly planned. The camps were generally poorly located and torture and punishment was a daily occurrence. Japan had never ratified the 1929 Prisoners of War Convention but had agreed to observe its provisions.

The railway was mostly dismantled after the war but there is a Buddhist Railway Museum at Kanchanaburi. All who died on the project were buried along the line and after the war the Army Graves Service transferred the graves to three main cemeteries. Kanchanaburi Cemetery where Edward George Grout is commemorated is the largest of the three war cemeteries and is situated close to the site of the former Kanburi base camp through which most of the prisoners passed on their way to other camps. It contains the graves of 7,000 POWs who worked along the southern section of the railway from Bangkok to Nieke.

CHAPTER 11

NORTH AFRICA 1942 – 43

The six month long Tunisian Campaign of 1942-43 against the Italian and German Armies ended the war in North Africa where there had been heavy fighting since the Italian invasion of Egypt in 1940. The Anglo American invasion of Tunisia in November 1942 hoped to cut off Field Marshal Rommel and his Panzerarmee Afrika which was retreating from the British Eighth Army in Libya. However there was a strong German build up around the ports of Tunis and Bizerte, which prevented a quick move to the east. There were initial deep penetrations of enemy lines but these were thrown back and throughout the winter the army held defensive positions.

There was fierce fighting in February when Rommel's forces attempted a breakthrough at Kasserine without success, and also throughout the spring of 1943. Lt. Roddy McLeod of Alderbury, later killed in Italy, was with the Scots Guards for their victory at the Battle of

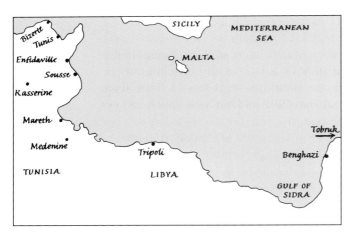

Medenine and also at Mareth where he was wounded. Tunis was captured on 7 May, and with the advance of the Eighth Army from the east and the increased effectiveness of the Allied blockade of the Mediterranean, enemy forces were short of fuel and supplies. On 13 May 250,000 Axis forces surrendered after the break-through at Enfidaville.

Arnold William Hatcher of Whaddon was killed on the last day of the Battle of Enfidaville in Tunisia. The Eighth Army had attacked the town on 13 April and Private Hatcher's battalion took over the front line on 23 April relieving the 7th Green Howards who had been involved in heavy fighting. The area was defended by German and Italian units who, despite being stranded without fuel and supplies, held out as long as possible. The Regimental History of The Queen's Royal Regiment records that the last twenty four hours before capitulation were notable for the greatly increased shelling as the Italians fired off their last stocks of ammunition. It was during this period that Private Hatcher was killed.

ARNOLD WILLIAM HATCHER
5729762 Private
2/5th Battalion The Queen's Royal Regiment
(West Surrey)
Died 12 May 1943. Aged 28.

Arnold William Hatcher was born on 15 May 1915, the son of Sidney and Edith Agnes Hatcher of Ladies Cottages, Whaddon. Before joining the army in 1940 he worked for Miss Fenn, the Baker at West Grimstead and then for six years as a conductor for the Wilts and Dorset Motor Services.

He enlisted into the Dorset Regiment in April 1940, just before his 25th birthday and was described as being 6ft tall and weighing 155 lbs. He joined The Queen's Royal Regiment and was posted to the 2/5th Battalion in August 1942.

The battalion embarked the Dutch liner *MV Johann van Oldenbarnvelt* shortly afterwards in Liverpool and set sail in convoy for an undisclosed destination (Iraq). The convoy which consisted of some 25 ships and destroyer escorts, zig zagged across the Atlantic for six weeks evading enemy submarines. Troops on the *Johann van Oldenbarnvelt* were able to carry out a daily one hour march on the wide decks. The convoy eventually arrived in Cape Town on 25 September. Unfortunately the Liberty boat *Ocean Flight* which contained most of their transport and guns had been torpedoed and sunk by a U Boat so consequently the battalion was temporarily non-operational. A short stay in Cape Town allowed the men to go ashore and enjoy fruit and bananas, which had not been seen at home since before the war.

They then transhipped to Bombay and spent two weeks at Deolali, a dusty camp outside the city before shipping to Basra where they arrived in the middle of November. Again they made camp in an arid dusty area until a train was available to take them via Baghdad to Kirkuk. Two uncomfortable and extremely cold nights were spent on the unheated train. On arrival in Kirkuk they met up with their new transport, which had travelled across the desert from Suez. Camp was established at Kirkuk and the troops began training and toughening up exercises. Local nomads were often near the camp and thieving was one of their pastimes so weapons and clothing had to be well safeguarded. From mid March 1943 the battalion followed the advance of the Eighth Army westwards across Libya via Tobruk, Benghazi and Tripoli. It arrived at a bivouac area 10 miles south of Enfidaville in Tunisia on 22 April 1943, almost exactly eight months after leaving Liverpool.

The journey from Kirkuk to Enfidaville, over 3,313 miles in 31 days, is documented by the regiment as the longest approach march in history. It is difficult to imagine nowadays the privations endured by the young soldiers en route to battle but an officer travelling in the battalion wrote:

For most of the last month I have been sharing a 3-tonner with 36 men under my command, being jolted and bumped over terrible roads, with cramped leg room and little opportunity to take exercise or relax. For the last few days we could hear the rumble of guns ahead, but when we stopped in the evening of the 22nd of April and were told that we would be moving into reserve positions in the line next morning, it was a surprise and a shock which we had not anticipated.

Arnold Hatcher travelled in this convoy of vehicles, was part of the battalion that took up the reserve behind the 2nd New Zealand Division outside Enfidaville and was on the line for three weeks. He was killed on the 12 May, the last day of the battle. A notice found in the Salisbury Times, 4 June 1943 states that Mrs Hatcher of Ladies Cottages, Whaddon had been informed that her youngest son Arnold aged 28 was killed in action on 12 May while serving with The Queens Royal Regiment (MP) section in North Africa. There is also a notification of death in the Killed on Active Service column of the Salisbury Times, 11 June 1943. The reference (MP) Military Police, on the telegram possibly refers to the fact that each battalion assigned soldiers to act as their own military policemen so it is possible he was one of these designated soldiers.

Pte Hatcher was awarded the War Medal 1939-45, the Defence Medal, the 1939-45 Star and the Africa Star with Eighth Army Clasp. He is buried in the Enfidaville War Cemetery, Tunisia, Reference VII.F.7. This cemetery is 100 km south of Tunis on the road to Zaghovan and marks the end of the Eighth Army's advance across North Africa. The men who are buried here died in the final battles from March to May 1943.

Africa Star

The final surrender of Axis forces in North Africa was completed with the Surrender Ceremony outside Enfidaville on 13 May 1945 which was arranged and overseen by the 2nd/7th Battalion of The Queen's Royal Regiment.

While researching Private Hatcher some interesting facts emerged concerning the troopship that transported him with his regiment to Cape Town.

THE JOHAN VAN OLDENBARNEVELT (THE LAKONIA)

The Johan van Oldenbarnevelt, which had one of the longest ships names in history, was built by The Netherlands Shipbuilding and Dry Dock Company of Amsterdam for the Netherlands Line in 1930. She was a 19,787 gross ton ship, length overall 609.2ft x beam 74.8ft, two funnels, two masts, twin screw and a speed of 19 knots. There was accommodation for 338 first class passengers, 281 second class, and 64-third class passengers. She was immediately chartered to Holland America Line for one Amsterdam to New York round trip.

During the five years from 1940-45, she was used as an Allied troopship and after the war was refitted as a one class vessel. In the 1950s she made eleven round voyages from Rotterdam to Quebec and Montreal while chartered to the The Netherlands Government, probably carrying emigrants. In 1958 she was rebuilt at Amsterdam to 20,314 tons with accommodation for 1,210 one-class passengers and on 2 April 1959 commenced her first round the world voyage from Amsterdam to Southampton, Suez, Australia, New Zealand, Panama Canal, Port Everglades, Bermuda, Southampton and Amsterdam. In total she made twelve round the world voyages on this route finishing in 1963.

She was then put up for sale and was bought by the Greek Line and renamed *Lakonia*. She sailed on a Christmas cruise to the Canary Islands from Southampton on 19 December 1963 after passing a Ministry of Transport safety inspection the previous day. She was carrying 646 passengers and 376 crew but unfortunately caught fire 200 miles NNE of Madeira on 22 December. Although many people were safely evacuated to Madeira, 128 lives were lost and the exact cause of the fire was never established. The ship was destroyed by fire and the hulk, which was being towed for salvage, sank on 29 December, 250 miles SW of Gibraltar.

CHAPTER 12

ITALY 1943

Following the end of the successful campaign in North Africa, the Allies implemented a three pronged invasion plan of southern Italy commencing on 3 September 1943. It was known that there were many German divisions in Italy and it has been suggested that Churchill may have seen the invasion of Italy as a means of drawing the German army away from France in preparation for D Day.

The operation which was codenamed BAYTOWN saw two divisions of the British Eighth Army, led by General Montgomery, cross the Straits of Messina and land at Reggio Calabria in the far south of Italy. There was little resistance from the Italian Army and the Italian Government, now under Marshall Pietro Badoglio since the fall of Mussolini in July, surrendered on 8 September. However, the large numbers of retreating German forces in the area devised numerous delaying tactics for the Allied army.

On 9 September the Allied Fifth Army under the Command of the American General Mark Clark landed at Salerno, south of Naples, and on the same day the British V Corps landed at Taranto on the east coast of Italy. After heavy fighting on many fronts these forces eventually joined together for a push to the north. The landings of British and American forces at Salerno on 9 September met immediate and heavy resistance from the occupying Germans and did not initially have sufficient back up forces to repel the German counter attack. There were heavy casualties.

Lt Roderick McLeod of Alderbury landed at Salerno and was killed two days later during the fierce fighting at the bridgehead established from the landing area.

RODERICK CAMPBELL McLEOD

186296 Lieutenant
2nd Battalion Scots Guards
Died 11 September 1943.
Aged 21.

Lt Roderick Campbell McLeod, or Roddy as he was known by friends and family, was born in Bath on 4 October 1921, the eldest son and heir of Sir Murdoch Campbell McLeod, 2nd Bt and Lady McLeod of Ashley Hill

House, Clarendon – Kelly's Directory for 1939 confirms that the family were resident there. He was educated at Winchester College and attested as a Rifleman into The King's Royal Rifle Corps at Southampton on 29 September 1939. His occupation was given as student and he was described as 5ft 11in tall and weighing 146lbs. He was placed in the Army Reserve, presumably because his age was under 18 years. After transferring to the Scots Guards he was posted to the Guards Depot at Pirbright for pre-commissioning training in November 1940. He attended the Officer Cadet Training Unit (OCTU) at Sandhurst and was commissioned a 2nd Lieutenant in the Scots Guards in 1941.

He initially joined the Training Battalion but in July 1942 he sailed from England to join the 2nd Battalion Scots Guards in the Middle East. The battalion had been sent to Syria in September 1942, after sixteen months fighting in the desert, to reform, rest and train and it was here that he joined them and was promoted to Lieutenant. In February 1943 they were ordered to the Western Desert and after an approach march of over 2,000 miles along the North African shore the battalion was in contact with the enemy at the Battle of Medenine. F Company, with Lt McLeod, held the centre of the line, which was 2,000 yards long. They defeated the German 21st Panzer Division by skilful use of their anti tank guns, knocking out many tanks. The battalion then moved up to attack the heavily defended Mareth Line and it was here, in March, as described in the Regimental History that Lt Mcleod was wounded whilst crossing a minefield, requiring hospitalisation and convalescence until mid June.

At the end of the North Africa Campaign the 2nd Battalion Scots Guards became part of the 5th Army X Corps formed for the invasion of Italy and commanded by General Mark Clark. The convoy transporting this Allied force sailed from Tripoli on the North African coast in the early morning of 5 September 1943. The battalion had converted from their artillery role to become an infantry unit and Lt McLeod rejoined F Company after his convalescence from wounds. The battalion was conveyed in a Landing Ship Tank (LST) and two Landing Craft Infantry (LCI) and a description of these craft from the

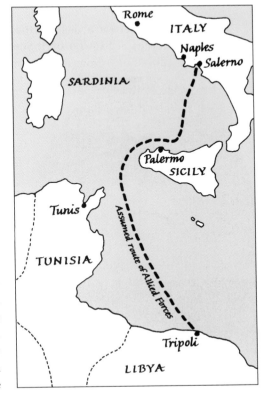

Tripoli to Salerno route

95

Regimental History illustrates the conditions under which the men were transported:

> *An L.C.I., like all beach craft has little grip on the water, and in such circumstances displays an agility wildly at variance with its squat and solid appearance. The low unbulwarked decks soon became uninhabitable and the misery in the airless crowded holds reached the point when men no longer have heart to grumble.*

The troops sat in the landing craft in blistering heat for nearly 48 hours while the convoy assembled and were then carried in cramped conditions for a further 24 hours or more as they crossed the open sea. They consoled themselves by being grateful to be leaving the hot fly-ridden desert. By 7 September the convoy was in more sheltered waters and was able to anchor beyond Palermo in Sicily where the men were allowed to swim. The next day course was laid for Salerno on the west coast of Italy with the landings planned for the early hours of 9 September. The Scots Guards as part of 201 Guards Brigade were to form part of the Corps Reserve and in the morning of that day reports state that:

> *........the Battalion sweltered in its landing craft about three or four miles off shore.*

They finally disembarked early in the afternoon and Lt. McLeod landed with F Company immediately south of the River Tusciano and moved about one mile inland to a holding area. That night they advanced to the Verdesca area south of the main Salerno to Battipaglia road.

The following morning, F Company moved up in support of the 6th Grenadiers who were engaging the enemy at the crossroads. The retreating Germans had taken advantage of the local terrain and left small parties of tanks and infantry concealed in the thick cover of drains and dykes. These waited until advancing Allied troops had passed and then began large scale sniping, causing many casualties. This tactic by the enemy was very effective and caused great disruption.

Salerno Bridgehead

The main objective of Lt McLeod's battalion was to secure the tobacco factory site on the main Salerno to Batipaglia road. The site commanded the enemy's main transverse supply route and consisted of a large agricultural storage depot with associated buildings covering about three and a half acres. (It was discovered later that the site was actually a tomato storage depot with canning plant attached.) The area was strongly defended, surrounded by eight feet high spiked railings and reinforced with wire.

On 11 September orders were received that the site was to be attacked that night as most of the enemy had apparently withdrawn. However, when the attack went ahead it was discovered that a battalion with tanks had secretly reinforced the site. Heavy fighting ensued over several days and battalion records state that as part of the attack on 11 September:

F Company with Lieut. Mcleod was on the left flank and directed on the main crossroads to the west of the Factory. The volume of Spandau fire from the crossroads was such that F Company was forced to withdraw after suffering heavy casualties including Lieutenant R.C McLeod, killed.

Portrait commissioned posthumously, courtesy of Scots Guards Museum.

It was not until 20 September that the beachhead at Salerno was finally stabilised and the battalion was able to advance.

Lt McLeod was initially recorded as buried at Pontecagnano Faiano but this was probably a field burial. His final resting place is in Salerno War Cemetery Italy, plot location 11.A.36. He is commemorated on both Alderbury memorials. His portrait and some of his personal effects, which were donated when the family house was cleared, are displayed at the Guards Museum, Wellington Barracks, London. The family believe his medals were claimed but stolen in a robbery.

With the establishment of the bridgehead at Salerno the campaign continued with a push towards Rome. The city was protected by the German Gustav Line, which had been carefully planned along the rivers Garigliano and Rapido and at Monte Cassino. It was extremely heavily fortified and held by fifteen German divisions under the command of General Kesselring. The line saw some of the fiercest fighting of the whole Italian Campaign.

CHAPTER 13

THE ROYAL AIR FORCE

Two men named on the Alderbury War Memorials, JWC Kidd and JW Snook, served in the RAF during World War II.

Following the evacuation of Dunkirk and the fall of France in 1940 the ground forces of Nazi Germany were stopped at the English Channel. Adolf Hitler launched an aerial bombardment over southern England to gain air superiority and open the way for an invasion. Luftwaffe heavy bombers escorted by fighter aircraft crossed the Channel every day to destroy ports, coastal defences, airfields and factories. The Battle of Britain was fought over the skies of southern England. Widespread damage occurred but the RAF pilots inflicted such heavy losses on the Luftwaffe that after 114 days of aerial combat, Germany conceded and withdrew its fighters. Prime Minister Winston Churchill paid tribute to the bravery of the aircrews of Fighter Command in a famous speech to the nation:

Never in the field of human conflict was so much owed by so many to so few.   20 August 1940

The next stage of the German offensive became known as The Blitz. On 7 September 1940 London suffered its first massive air raid by over 300 German bombers. Eight days later more than 400 German aircraft attacked London. Anti-aircraft fire and the skill of the RAF fighter pilots again inflicted such heavy losses that large scale German daylight operations were halted. The next phase, which the Germans sustained for 57 consecutive nights, was night raids over London with high explosive and incendiary bombs. Other cities and ports throughout the British Isles were also heavily bombed as were manufacturing and industrial areas in this attempt to cut the country's lifelines. The attacks continued to the middle of 1941 when German attention was concentrated on gathering together military resources for the attack on Soviet Russia.

The survival of Britain was due to the indomitable spirit of the people who refused to give in despite the massive destruction of their towns and cities and to the bravery of the RAF fighter crews and those who manned the anti aircraft guns and searchlights. Despite having only six squadrons of dedicated night fighters and 2,000 anti aircraft guns the RAF broke the back of the Luftwaffe offensive.

During this time aircraft of Coastal Command patrolled the Atlantic Ocean, protecting convoys from enemy attack. John Walter Cameron

Kidd, whose parents moved to Alderbury at the beginning of the war, flew with Coastal Command as a pilot and was killed in December 1942.

JOHN WALTER CAMERON KIDD
913390 Sergeant
Royal Air Force Volunteer Reserve
Died 06 December 1942. Aged 21.

John Kidd was born on 14 March 1921 in Yorkshire where his father worked as a coachman groom. The family moved several times and John attended Malmesbury Secondary School before joining the RAF at 17 years of age in 1938. John's parents and twin sisters moved to Alderbury when his father became Head Groom at Longford Park and they lived in part of Rose Cottage, Silver Street. Although John never lived in Alderbury he was a frequent visitor during his leaves. His family tell us that he trained as an RAF pilot in Canada. He flew a Hudson Mk1 bomber in 224 Squadron, RAF Coastal Command protecting Atlantic Convoys and they remember him saying that his aircraft sank a German E Boat.

The Hudson bomber, which carried a crew of five, was manufactured by Lockheed and used by the RAF for sea patrol reconnaissance. It distinguished itself in combat against German submarines. The family tell us that in 1939 John was flying out of Prestwick and in 1942 he was probably due for posting to the Middle East. However, they were informed that on 6 December 1942 his plane crashed and all the crew were lost. With the help of the Air Historical Branch (RAF), it has been possible to piece together the background to Sergeant Kidd's tragic accident.

As 1942 drew to a close, a massive effort was underway to prepare for Operation TORCH, the major Allied offensive in the Middle East. Many of the aircraft that were to take part in the Operation were flown out by crews from No. 1 Overseas Aircraft Despatch Unit at RAF Portreath in Cornwall. On 6 December 1942, Sergeant Kidd and his crew were detailed to ferry a Hudson Mk VI (serial number FK522) from Portreath to Gibraltar. They got airborne at 5.25am, and climbed to 1,700 feet in a left-hand circuit. During the turn, the aircraft gradually lost height and hit cliffs at Nighton Beach, exploding. Just one body was recovered. Only five minutes earlier, another aircraft, Beaufort DD980, had crashed nearby, seemingly in similar circumstances. A total of nine aircrew died in the two crashes. Although John's planned eventual destination is not recorded, it seems that the flight to Gibraltar might well have been the first leg of a deployment, as his family has long believed, to North Africa.

He was awarded the 1939-45 War Medal and the Atlantic Star. He is commemorated on the Alderbury memorials and Panel 87 of the Runnymede Memorial. He is also remembered in the church at Sherston, near Malmesbury, where he lived as a boy.

THE RUNNYMEDE MEMORIAL

The Runnymede Memorial overlooks the River Thames near Windsor and contains the names of over 20,000 airmen who were lost in World War II and have no known grave. It was designed by Sir Edward Maufe with sculpture by Vernon Hill. The engraved glass and painted ceilings were designed by John Hutton, who also designed the glass in the Dunkirk Memorial and the Great West Screen in the new Coventry Cathedral. The poem engraved on the gallery window was written by Paul H Scott. From the top of the Memorial it is possible to see the modern Heathrow Airport.

During World War II a strategic air offensive over Germany and occupied Europe was sustained for five years at heavy cost including the lives of over 55,000 airmen in Bomber Command alone. Throughout 1943 the RAF bombed cities in Germany at night whilst the Americans bombed during daylight. Bombing raids kept many German men on anti aircraft duties who would otherwise have been on front line service. Raids were aimed at the industrial heartland of Germany to weaken munitions production and interrupt the chain of supplies to the front lines.

Jack William Snook of Alderbury was killed in a bombing raid over Germany in 1943.

JACK WILLIAM SNOOK
161695 Pilot Officer
90 Squadron, Royal Air Force Volunteer Reserve
Died 19 November 1943. Aged 25.

Jack Snook was born in Salisbury on 2 October 1918 and, when he was eight years old he moved to Alderbury with his family. The family who lived in Firs Road consisted of his parents, William and Ada, his sister Marjorie and his brother Eric. He attended Alderbury School and later, Bishop Wordsworth's Grammar School in Salisbury. His sister remembers that he was a very keen sportsman like his father who was a founder member of Alderbury Bowls Club. He had a Saturday job at Occomore's Bakery, now the Whaddon Post Office and joined the Post Office Engineering Department in February 1937. The Post Office at that time had responsibility for the telephone system so he may have worked in that section as an engineer.

He joined the Portsmouth Police Force in July 1938 when he was 19 years old and just under six feet tall with blue eyes and brown hair. After initial training he was posted to B Division and in November 1940 he was promoted to the CID and sent for training. During his time in the Portsmouth Police Force he received two Commendations, one from the Salisbury Police for his assistance during a disturbance in the city and the other from the Chief Constable of Portsmouth for keen observation, zeal and initiative in connection with an arrest.

He enlisted in the RAF Volunteer Reserve (RAFVR) on 10 April 1941 and his sister Marjorie says he trained as a navigator in America and Canada. He met his wife at Scarborough in 1943 when he was converting onto the Stirling Bomber at a nearby Operational Training Unit. Records show that he was awarded a Commission for the Emergency as a Pilot Officer in the General Duties branch of the RAFVR on 28 September 1943. His family tells us that he flew over 20 operations in Stirling bombers and was due for leave after his last mission.

At 5.10pm on 18 November 1943 he took off from Wratting Common at West Wickham aboard Stirling Mark III EH996 WP-H destination Mannheim/Ludwigshafen in Germany. There were 395 bombers on that raid including 114 Stirlings of which 17 were from 90 Squadron at Wratting. The force attacked effectively in difficult weather but more importantly appears to have diverted many of the German night fighters away from Berlin, which was then attacked by a further force of 440

Lancaster bombers. On the return leg of the raid Jack Snook's plane was listed as having crashed at Fussgonheim some 10km WSW of Ludwigshafen. Seven of the crew of eight were killed including Jack Snook and one of the crew, Sgt E Northard, was taken POW. Two Stirlings from 90 Squadron were lost on the mission although the Squadron History does not record this. The Stirling bomber played a major part in the strategic offensive of the RAF over Germany as it could fly long distances carrying very heavy bomb loads.

Jack Snook was survived by his wife and a daughter born after his death. He is commemorated on both Alderbury memorials. He is also commemorated on the Bishop Wordsworth School Memorial, the Portsmouth Police Roll of Honour and 90 Squadron Roll of Honour in Tuddenham St Mary's Church, Cambridgeshire, the home of 90 Squadron. He is buried at Rheinberg War Cemetery in Germany. The majority of those buried there are fallen airmen brought in from numerous German cemeteries in the area.

90 SQUADRON

Formed in October 1917 the squadron was initially equipped with Sopwith Dolphin single seat fighter aircraft for use in France. However, it was not sent overseas and was disbanded in August 1918. Eleven days later it was reformed as a Home Defence unit and equipped with Sopwith Camels and Avro 504s until again disbanded in 1919, after the end of World War I.

In 1937, prior to the outbreak of World War II, the squadron was reformed. This time as a bomber unit equipped with the Hawker Hind and Bristol Blenheim Mark I. In May 1941 it was selected as the first RAF Squadron to receive the Boeing B-17 Flying Fortress aircraft from America. These were used for high altitude day bombing missions over Germany.

In November 1942, as a heavy bomber squadron equipped with Stirlings, it made a significant contribution to the attack on Hamburg and the famous raid on Peenemunde. It was also involved in major attacks in the Ruhr regions of Germany and mine laying operations. Lancaster bombers eventually replaced the Stirling and the squadron continued to play a major part in Bomber Command offensives until late 1945. The Squadron finally disbanded in 1965.

From 1944 – 45 Allied fighters swept the skies of Europe and bombers attacked road and rail movements, tank columns and airfields ahead of the advancing Allied land forces. Bombing raids continued on major targets within the German heartland until the surrender of Germany.

CHAPTER 14

WESTERN EUROPE 1944 – 45

From June 1940 France was under German occupation and, apart from infiltration by Special Agents of the SOE and the occasional raid, no Allied soldier set foot on French soil until 6 June 1944. Both the Allies and Germany were aware that the decisive struggle in Western Europe must come from an invasion.

For two years the Allies worked on invasion plans and built up supplies along the south coast of England. By May 1944 a total of 47 divisions of Allied soldiers were equipped and waiting for the final command to launch the invasion of France codenamed OVERLORD. False information deliberately placed by the intelligence services misled the German Army to the time, location and importance of the landings. The German forces were dispersed and their subsequent attempts at concentration and resupply were thwarted by the effective sabotage campaign of the French Resistance and constant Allied air attack.

The Invasion Plan

The assaulting force was carried to France by a fleet of more than 4,000 vessels under the command of Admiral Bertram Ramsey who had also co-ordinated and commanded the Dunkirk evacuation fleet in 1940. The Commander in Chief of OVERLORD was the American, General Eisenhower, who directed the Supreme Headquarters. The ground forces were commanded by General Montgomery of the British Army.

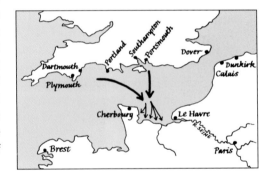

D DAY LANDINGS

The invasion of France was launched on 6 June 1944, a date that has gone down in history as D Day. On that day Allied forces landed in Normandy in the largest ever combined operation and amphibious landing. It was made possible only by Allied control of the air and sea. Fighter aircraft and bombers flew over 14,000 sorties in the first twenty four hours, targeting German coastal defences.

The landings took place at dawn on a 50 mile stretch of the Normandy coastline from Caen westwards and large numbers of self-propelled barges allowed soldiers to get out as quickly as possible in the shallow waters of the beaches. Infantry divisions assaulted five beaches

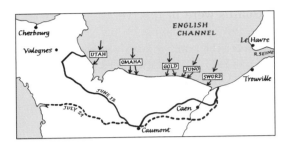

Normandy Beaches and Bridgehead

codenamed Sword, Juno, Gold, Omaha and Utah. All were heavily defended and there were many casualties. Close air support and naval bombardment supported the infantry and by nightfall of D Day all the landing sites had established beachheads.

During the next few weeks of continuous heavy fighting all these units eventually met up to form one front which was supported by landings of further combat troops. Sub Lt. Stanley Gumbleton from Whaddon, who was killed later in the campaign, was aboard *HMS Forester* carrying support troops to the D Day beaches.

Despite a determined defence by the Germans, by mid June, the Allies had penetrated well inland from the Normandy beaches on a 60 mile front. The Breakout from Normandy started on 25 July and Lt Michael Christie-Miller of Clarendon Park was killed at the Battle of Caumont during The Breakout.

MICHAEL VANDELEUR CHRISTIE-MILLER
207659 Lieutenant
Coldstream Guards
Died 30 July 1944. Aged 22.

Born in 1922, Michael was the youngest son of Mr and Mrs SR Christie-Miller of Clarendon Park. He was educated at Eton and after leaving school he worked at the Experimental Station at Porton under Sir Joseph Barcroft. During this time he formed the Clarendon section of the Home Guard. He attested as a Guardsman into the Coldstream Guards on 3 April 1941 giving his occupation as student. He was 5ft 11in tall and weighed 145lbs.

He was recommended for commissioning and, after attending OCTU, was commissioned a 2nd Lieutenant in the Coldstream Guards and posted to the Guards Training Battalion at Pirbright. From there he joined the 4th (Motor) Battalion Coldstream Guards and was promoted to lieutenant on 1 October 1942. The battalion had switched from its traditional infantry role in 1941 and was equipped with Churchill tanks.

On D Day, the 4th Battalion Coldstream Guards were in reserve as part of the 6th Guards Armoured Brigade. They left for France on 19 July from an embarkation area near Southampton Water. The tanks were driven onto LCTs for an uneventful, calm crossing. Early on 20 July the tanks rolled off onto Juno and Gold beaches, moved inland and concentrated in orchards in the vicinity of Bayeux. The area was clear of enemy shelling and they remained there for one week in reserve.

On Friday 28 July they advanced in preparation for battle in front of Caumont where a strong enemy force was holding up the American advance down the Cherbourg peninsula. The 6th Guards Tank Brigade that included the Coldstreams was supported by the 15th Scottish Division.

Michael Christie-Miller is listed as part of the Headquarters Squadron but on the day of his death he was attached to No 3 Company as Squadron Rear Link with responsibility for communications to Battalion HQ. No 3 Squadron Coldstream tanks advanced along the Caumont to St. Martin road to attack Hill 309, and the Regimental history records:

> No 3 squadron ran into the enemy at the small village of La Morichesse, so the Commanding Officer decided to turn east and make straight across country to Hill 309. A little later Lieut. Christie-Miller who had been travelling some distance behind and had not heard of the diversion as he was in the spare Rear-Link tank, went straight on into the village of La Morichesse, and was knocked out by a Panther at 200 yards range, he and 2 members of his crew were killed.

Friends of his report that he was separated from the group because of engine trouble with his tank and it is also possible that his wireless may not have been in working order and he did not receive the message to divert.

He is buried at St. Charles de Percy War Cemetery to the north of Vire in Normandy, Grave V.D.9. The CWGC states that this cemetery is the south-ernmost of the Normandy cemeteries and the majority of the 809 burials are of those killed in late July and early August 1944 in the major thrust to drive a wedge between the German 7th Army and Panzer Group West. He is commemorated on the Alderbury memorials and the Eton College War Memorial. He was awarded the War Medal 1939-45, the Defence Medal, the 1939-45 Star and the France and Germany Star.

Allied forces were victorious at the Battle of Caumont, described as the first and finest battle for the Guards Tank Brigade, few of whose men had been in action before. Guardsman Cyril Witt of Alderbury, killed in 1945 also belonged to this regiment and fought in this battle.

TANKS

The tanks used by the Coldstream Guards were Churchill tanks, manufactured in Luton by Vauxhall and served by a crew of five. After the Dunkirk evacuation in 1940, the British Army had only about 100 tanks left and a new tank was designed, developed and built in just under 12 months. The Churchill first entered service in 1941, was well armoured, mechanically reliable and had a relative high top speed of 17mph with a range of 90 miles. It had a very good turning ability and strong suspension and chassis which enabled it to be modified for a number of specialised uses such as assaults on fortified positions, and as carpet layers and flame throwers. The Churchill was outgunned by it's German counterpart but had a thick protective armour. A total of 5,640 Churchills, versions Mark I-VII, were manufactured.

The tanks used by the German Army in Normandy were Panther tanks. For the first few years of the World War II and especially for Blitzkrieg strategy, the German army had used the Panzer tanks versions I-IV. After the successful resistance to this tank by the Red Army during the Russian Campaign a new tank had to be commissioned. The Panther entered service in November 1942 and between 1942-5 Germany produced 4,814 Panther tanks. The tank had a 650hp engine and 75mm armour-penetrating gun. With sloped armour to deflect shot, torsion bar suspension and interleaved road wheels, it could travel at 28mph.

The Battle of Normandy ended in mid August 1944 with the complete defeat of the German forces in the area. Today, travellers to Normandy can drive *La route de la Victoire*, so designated by the French Government as "The Road To Freedom" with specially designed victory kilometre markers. On 25 August, Paris was liberated and German forces withdrew further north. In southern France in mid August, American and French Divisions landed on the Mediterranean coasts causing the German troops in that area to retreat up the Rhone Valley where they were severely harassed by the French Resistance.

The breakout across the River Seine from Paris sent the German Army into retreat across northern France and into Belgium. The Americans advanced on the right, the British Second Army went up the centre of Europe to liberate Brussels and Antwerp, and the Canadian First Army fought its way up the coast liberating the Channel Ports.

On 4 September 1944 the Allies under General Montgomery took the important Belgian port of Antwerp. The intention was to use the port as a

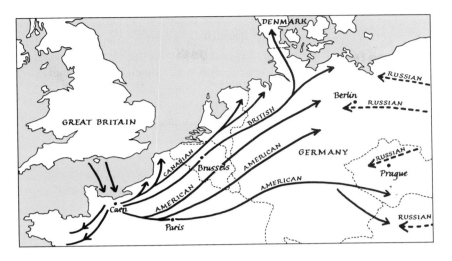

Progress of advance.

supply base for the invasion of Germany but a tactical error occurred when they failed to secure the estuary approach. As a result, that part of Belgium was the focus of heavy fighting throughout the latter part of 1944. In this area Private Jack Attwood Woodrow from Alderbury died.

JACK ATTWOOD WOODROW
5826259 Private
Ist Battalion The Suffolk Regiment
Died 30 December 1944. Aged 25.

Jack Woodrow came from a family closely involved with the military as depicted in the photograph. The family members are from left to right, – Father and Uncle Joseph (sitting) – Arthur, Frank, William and Jack (standing).

Jack Woodrow was born on the 20 December 1919 at Ventnor, Isle of Wight where his father owned the Star Inn at Knighton. His father, William Archibald Woodrow, had landed in France with the Old Contemptibles in 1914 and

was blinded by shrapnel during the retreat from Mons. He was trained by St Dunstan's, the charity for blind servicemen, as a poultry farmer. The family moved to Ebbesbourne Wake and the poultry farm was in their back garden. As a St Dunstaner he used the skill of netting, which they had also taught him, for his World War II effort making camouflage nets.

Jack's brothers Arthur, Frank and William were all in the forces and his sister Elizabeth (known as Betty) who had attended school in Alderbury was in the WAAF. Jack's old friend Leslie Foyle of Ebbesbourne Wake, where they both attended school, remembers him as a lively fun loving boy who was always ready for a laugh. He provided a photo of Jack at 14 years of age just before he joined up. Frank tells us that their parents moved to The Gables on Southampton Rd, Alderbury to:

.......enable members of the family coming home on leave to make the last leg of the journey a reasonable one. At least within walking distance from Salisbury station as transport was not readily available in those days, particularly when time was most important.

Jack was living with his parents in Ebbesbourne Wake when he enlisted in The Suffolk Regiment as a Band Boy on 24 April 1934. He was 14 years old, 5ft 3in tall and weighed 112lbs. He trained as a bassoonist at the Royal Military School of Music and went with the regiment to Malta in 1939 and from there to India, probably to Rasmak on the NW Frontier.

He was trained as a First Aider and Stretcher Bearer, this being a tradition for members of military bands. He returned to the UK in March 1944 and remained with the 1st Suffolks until he was transferred to the 2nd/7th Warwicks in June 1944. This regiment was located in Dover at that time and was responsible for looking after the returning wounded from the D Day invasion, so Jack was not with the Ist Suffolks when they landed in France. The Suffolks were involved in heavy fighting in NW Europe until December by which time they were holding the Maas River Line. Jack rejoined them at this time and died on the 30 December 1944 in a field ambulance unit of heart failure following infective hepatitis.

Jack is buried at Ronse (Reniax) Communal Cemetery, Oost-Vlaanderen. Belgium, Grave A7 and commemorated on the Alderbury memorials. He was awarded the India General Service Medal with the 1937-39 Clasp, the War Medal 1939-45, the Defence Medal, The 1939-45 Star, the Burma Star and the France and Germany Star.

The war in Europe continued through 1945 and the great success of the Allied assault on the Rhine signalled the beginning of the end of German resistance. By late April 1945 the Coldstream Guards, as part of the 6th Guards Armoured Brigade, had fought their way through France, Belgium and Holland and had reached the River Elbe near Lavenburg in Germany. Cyril Witt had been with the battalion throughout this time and it was during fighting to cross the River Elbe that he was killed on 1 May 1945.

CYRIL WITT
2661185 Guardsman
4th Batallion, Coldstream Guards
Died 1 May 1945. Aged 29.

Cyril Witt was the son of William Day Witt and Winifred Blanche Witt of Fordingbridge. He was one of three brothers who lived in Alderbury, his brothers Ralph and Fred survived the war.

He was born on 16 July 1915 at Poole, but is recorded as living with his wife and daughter in Wimborne when he enlisted with the Coldstream Guards in Southampton in April 1940. He was posted to the 4th (Motor) Battalion Coldstream Guards and served with them as a Driver/Operator. He was in the same battalion as Lt. Christie-Miller, landed in France and was involved in the Battle for Caumont in the Normandy Breakout. He remained with the regiment as it fought its way northwards.

By April 1945 they had reached the River Elbe in Germany where a Class 40 bridge had been quickly built across the river. The Coldstream Guards were instructed to cross the bridge to lend support to the bridgehead. The enemy was trying desperately to destroy the bridge and kept up a spasmodic bombardment all day. The Regimental History records that one salvo landed right beside one of the tanks that had broken down and was at the riverside. The crew of five men were all seriously wounded and died later in hospital. Cyril Witt is named as one of this crew. He died of wounds at 15 (British) Field Ambulance on 1 May 1945, and the next day the breakout towards Lubeck was complete.

He was awarded the War Medal 1939-45, the Defence Medal, the 1939-45 Star and the France and Germany Star. He is buried at Becklingen War Cemetery, Germany, grave ref. 17.F.12. The site of this cemetery is 13km south east of Soltau on the Hamburg to Hanover road overlooking Luneburg Heath where the final German surrender was taken. The majority of the 2,500 graves are those of soldiers who were killed during the final two months of the war. The other graves are those of soldiers brought in from isolated burials within a 50 mile radius. Luneburg Heath was the pre war training ground of the German army and the infamous Belsen Concentration Camp lies about eight miles to the south.

At the end of April 1945 the Soviet Armies, advancing from the East met the Allied Armies advancing from the West at the River Elbe and Germany was effectively cut in half. The German surrender was taken at Luneburg Heath on 8 May 1945.

CHAPTER 15

THE ROYAL NAVY

German attempts to blockade Britain by preventing delivery of goods and supplies led to the Atlantic Ocean becoming a battlefield. Mines were dropped in shipping lanes. Long range German bombers from coastal Europe attacked the ships that were bringing much needed food and supplies from America to Britain. The German Navy fleets of surface raiders and U Boats were a constant danger. The attacks were intensified after the fall of France and the losses to the British Merchant Fleet became very heavy, over 700,000 tons of shipping in 1940-41 alone.

In July 1941 Britain introduced a convoy system to escort merchant ships across the Atlantic. These convoys consisted of Royal Navy destroyers, corvettes and aircraft from small carriers. At first losses remained high, but by 1942 the convoys had become stronger and more skilful at locating the packs of U-Boats that hunted them and were better equipped with radar and aircraft.

An extension to the Battle of the Atlantic in 1941 involved sending Arctic convoys to supply the hard pressed Russian forces. These convoys sailed to the ports of Archangel and Murmansk carrying fuel, ammunition and vehicles. There were many losses but sufficient supplies got through to make a difference. The Battle of the Atlantic reached its climax in early 1943 when Germany had over 200 U Boats in action. Ship sinkings were high but successful destruction of the U Boats by combined Allied air and sea forces led to the remainder being recalled to Germany in the early summer. Allied air attacks on the German battleship raiders eliminated them one by one and the last remaining, the *Tirpitz*, was destroyed in 1944. This marked the end of the Battle of the Atlantic.

During these years the German Navy was also active in the Mediterranean, attacking convoys and troopships. The Royal Navy defended valiantly with many losses on both sides.

Stanley Gumbleton from Whaddon served in The Royal Navy aboard the destroyer *HMS Forester*.

STANLEY KENNETH GUMBLETON
Sub Lieutenant
HMS Forester
Died 23 July 1944. Aged 22.

Stanley Gumbleton came from Burcombe to live in Whaddon with his parents, Walter and Mary Gumbleton, when he was 14 years old. He had one sister called Gwendoline Norah and she tells us that the family lived at The Pines, one of four bungalows situated near the disused sandpit. He also had a half brother called Percy, who served in the Merchant Navy, and a half sister called Elsie. Their father was a retired Metropolitan policeman recalled by his family as very authoritarian and against Stanley joining the navy.

Stanley joined the Royal Navy in August 1937 as a '*Boy Second Class at 9 pence a day*' at *HMS St Vincent* in Gosport. He first went to sea in November 1938 and his Midshipman's log shows that he served aboard *HMS Ramilies*, travelling from Aden to Australia and New Zealand and back via Madagascar and Cape Town. His family have Crossing the Equator Certificates from this time showing he crossed the line in 1939 and again in December 1941. From May to November 1943 he was at the land based *HMS Collingwood* in Fareham and was commissioned as an officer from there. He wrote that the new officers were given an allowance for kit for service in war conditions and that he had been able to buy himself a pair of half-wellington boots.

Stanley Gumbleton

He joined *HMS Forester*, a destroyer in Western Approaches Command, serving as part of the Close Escort Group for Atlantic Convoys. He would have seen action with the ship as support was given to the hard pressed Atlantic Convoys and it is recorded that on 10 March 1944 *Forester* was involved in the sinking of the German U Boat *U845*. *Forester* was withdrawn from convoy duty in May 1944 to form part of the D Day Fleet for the Allied invasion of France. She was on duty carrying follow-up troops from 6 June until 3 July for the assault, and afterwards protecting supply convoys to the landing grounds. On 23 July 1944 *Forester* was engaged with enemy forces off the French coast early in the morning and according to a letter written by the Captain to the family:

> *Sub Lieutenant Gumbleton was at his action stations on the bridge, controlling the fire of starshells to illuminate the enemy. His illumination was most effective and enabled the ships other guns to inflict definite damage on the enemy. But an enemy shell hit the bridge and he was hit in the head. He was killed instantly.*

111

A letter Stanley had written to his parents on 14 July was delivered after his death. He wrote that they need not have been worried about the naval losses during the Normandy invasion because: *it was safer crossing to Normandy than crossing a road.* He also warned them not to expect him home on leave for some time as:

> *bringing a destroyer in harbour to give leave means less protection for the soldiers, which means the U-boats have a chance. So don't worry, because I shall just walk in one day and I expect mum will say"Two small ones please" or "Not today thank you" and that will be that.*

War medal
Atlantic Star
39-45 Star

Letter from
King Geoge

He is buried at Haslar Naval Cemetery, Portsmouth. Grave G.10.27 and commemorated on the Alderbury memorials. He is also commemorated on a brass plaque at Burcombe Church, Salisbury.

For Christmas 1942 Stanley Gumbleton received a Christmas card from friends in New Zealand with a verse that illustrated their feelings and support for the Mother Country.

BUCKINGHAM PALACE

The Queen and I offer you our heartfelt sympathy in your great sorrow.

We pray that your country's gratitude for a life so nobly given in its service may bring you some measure of consolation.

George R.I.

Mrs. M. Gumbleton.

> *Britannia's fight in Freedom's cause*
> *Shall not be fought alone.*
> *Her children of the southern Seas*
> *Rush to the battle zone.*
> *The Golden Age of Liberty*
> *Will dawn in Victory when*
> *Wars evil deeds are replaced by*
> *Peace on earth, Goodwill to men.*

HMS FORESTER

HMS Forester, a destroyer of the Fearless class, was built and engined by JS White & Co. Ltd of Cowes, Isle of Wight, launched in June 1934 and completed in April 1935. Before the outbreak of war she served as part of the Home Fleet based at Portsmouth and in 1939 moved to Scapa Flow for Coastal defence and anti submarine duties.

On 26 June 1940 *Forester* left Scapa to join Force 8 based on Gibraltar and was immediately in action against German submarines. In September she took part in Operation MENACE which was an unsuccessful attempt to capture Dakar by the Free French. Dakar was an important Naval Base in Senegal, West Africa. In November she took part with Force H in Operation COLLAR, escorting the passage of an Allied convoy through the Mediterranean and engaging the Italian Fleet off Cape Spartivento with great success. Further duties included resupply to the Army of the Nile, operations for the reinforcement of fighter aircraft for Malta and the guarding of supply convoys for the relief of Malta.

Late 1941 saw *Forester* relocate for Atlantic Convoy escort duty where she won Battle Honours. In May 1942 she was damaged whilst escorting an Arctic convoy from Iceland to Murmansk. After repairs she continued with convoy escort duty until 1944. She supported the Invasion on escort duty with Personnel Convoy ETP1 from the Thames carrying follow-up troops. She then returned for coastal duties and in late 1945 she entered the Reserve Fleet.

CHAPTER 16

SERVING PERSONNEL WHO DIED IN UK DURING WORLD WAR II

This section remembers the lives of those serving personnel who did not die in Theatres of War but on home soil.

SAMUEL ALEXANDER HOLWELL KIRKBY MC
Colonel
The Royal Sussex Regiment
Died 28 May 1943. Aged 45.

Grave 160 in Alderbury churchyard is the last resting place of Colonel SAH Kirkby MC who was killed in a road traffic accident whilst returning to Military HQ at Longford Castle on Friday 28 May 1943. There are no records or photographs of his funeral as events at that time, preparations for D Day, were shrouded in secrecy. However, his daughter was told by her mother that her father was on General Montgomery's staff and the funeral was a very large military ceremony with four generals present. There is a letter in the Longford Castle archives from General Montgomery to the Countess of Radnor confirming he used the castle as his HQ at this time.

Colonel Kirkby was born on 10 December 1898 in County Cork where his Yorkshire father was working as an engineer. He was educated at Dulwich College and commissioned from the Royal Military College to the 2nd Battalion, The Royal Sussex Regiment in 1917 to serve immediately on the Western Front. As a 2nd Lieutenant at 18 years of age he was awarded the Military Cross for gallantry. The citation in the London Gazette (edition 31480) states:

During an attack on the enemy near Pontru on 18th September 1918 he showed great gallantry and skill in handling his platoon, on one occasion going and assisting another company to repulse an enemy counter-attack. During the second attack at midnight, when all the other officers of the company were killed, he assumed command and conducted the fighting with conspicuous gallantry, and made disposi-

tions in a difficult situation to withstand possible enemy counter-attack.

The battalion had held the front line from 16 September, with a frontage of 1,100 yards. The Regimental War Diaries describe the action as: *a major assault on enemy positions to the north and south of Vandencourt on the 18 September as part of the major offensive by the 3rd and 4th Armies.*

He returned to England in 1919 and between the wars held several Staff Appointments including ADC to the Governor of the Straits Settlements. There are many photographs of him in the Regimental Albums on official duties and at ceremonials.

In 1939 he was posted with the BEF to France with the rank of acting Lt Col. He served at HQ and was in charge of Lines of Communication. He received an MID (Mentioned in Dispatches) at the retreat to Dunkirk (London Gazette 20 December 1940). Army records of the exact events have been lost but it is known that he was with the 6th Battalion on the second troop train. The first troop train carrying the 1st Battalion was severely depleted by Luftwaffe attack with only 300 men surviving. According to family information he was one of the last to leave the beaches. He landed in Falmouth on 18 June 1940, as reported in a letter to his Regimental Depot which advised his safe return and intention of reporting for duty as soon as possible.

After Dunkirk he was posted in charge of the defence of Orkney and Shetland until 1942. Subsequently he was appointed to the Staff post of Colonel in Charge of Administration for the Hants & Dorset District HQ, a sub group of Southern Command, based at Longford Castle near Salisbury.

On 28 May 1943 he and two other officers were travelling in a Staff car driven by an NCO when it was in collision with a tank towing a bren gun carrier which broke loose on a corner. The impact killed Col Kirkby instantly. He left a widow, a son Keith, and a daughter Anne. There are now five grandchildren and eight great grandchildren.

For WWI he was awarded the Military Cross, British War Medal 1917 and the Victory Medal. For WWII he was awarded the 1939-45 Star with Oakleaf, the British War Medal and the Defence Medal. He is commemorated on Dulwich College Roll of Honour.

His grave in Alderbury churchyard does not have a CWGC headstone as the family had initially requested a private memorial. However, as a result of this research project an inspector of the CWGC visited the grave and recommended regular inspections. In July 2004 family members who had been contacted during the research visited the grave. After discussions it was agreed that they would follow up the contact with the CWGC and request an official headstone. Only family members are allowed this privilege.

SIDNEY CHARLES MITCHELL
14543185 Private
General Service Corps
Died 13 May 1943. Aged 18.

G.S.C.

Sidney Charles Mitchell was born 7 October 1924 at Pitton where he lived with his brother John and parents, Mr and Mrs Arthur Mitchell at Four Cottages on the Clarendon Estate. His occupation at enlistment was house painter and his father worked as a woodsman on the Clarendon Estate where he and his son are still remembered.

He joined the General Service Corps as a Private on 18 February 1943. The General Service Corps was an administrative non-combat unit. Two months after joining up, while in training with his unit he fell ill. He died of encephalitis in Horton Emergency Hospital near Epsom on 13 May 1943.

He is buried in St Peter's Church Cemetery, Pitton and listed on the Alderbury memorials.

CHARLES EDWARD TURNER
1566399 Bombardier
Royal Regiment of Artillery
Died 1946. Aged 33.

Charles Edward Turner, or Charlie as he was known by his family, was born on 17 August 1912 at West Grimstead. He was a brick-maker by trade, working with his brother Harry for Mr Hand at the Whaddon Brickworks. His father William was a keeper at Longford Park and the family lived in a cottage at Knightwood. Charlie had attended East Grimstead School with his three brothers, Harry, Bill and Phil and his three sisters Annie, Effie and Ivy. As he grew older, Charlie became a very keen darts player and could often be found with one of his brothers playing darts in the Spring Cottage Pub at West Grimstead. It is not quite clear when the family moved to The Meadows in Whaddon but Phil's wife recalls they were living there well before the war broke out.

Charles Turner, in uniform with his brother Philip Turner, 1940

Charlie enlisted in the Royal Artillery on 15 August 1940 when he was 28 years old and by then he was 5ft 9in tall and weighed 145lbs. After training he was posted to 353 HYAA (Heavy Anti-Aircraft) Battery and promoted to Lance Bombardier in May 1941 and to Bombardier in March 1944. In September 1940, 353 Battery was formed as part of the 112th Regiment RA (TA) and he served with it in mainland Britain until D Day.

The battery boarded landing craft in Southend and Charlie landed with them in France on 9 June 1944, D Day+3. They were under the command of 76AA Brigade throughout the campaign across NW Europe and he was with them in Kapellen, Netherlands in May 1945 at the cessation of hostilities. In June 1945 he was posted to the Y List (long term ill) and was later medically discharged from the army on 21 October 1945. He was not in the services when he died of cancer in 1946. He is however commemorated on the Alderbury War Memorial and buried in Grave 144 in St Mary's churchyard Alderbury.

He is recorded as being awarded the War Medal 1939-45, but may also have been eligible for the Defence Medal, the 1939-45 Star and the France and Germany Star.

WILLIAM FOSTER GC MC DCM
Lieutenant
Home Guard
Died 13 September 1942. Aged 62.

William Foster, the oldest direct recipient of the George Cross, is buried in grave 164 in Alderbury churchyard. The grave is marked with a CWGC headstone bearing the George Cross insignia.

He was born at sea on 12 December 1880 when his father, Colour Sergeant George Foster of the Royal Marine Light Infantry, was returning from a period of duty in West Africa. He joined The Royal Fusiliers at entry age to serve in the Boer War. He was transferred to the 2nd Imperial Light Horse, a South African regiment, badly wounded in action and sent back to the UK, where he was discharged as medically unfit in 1902, aged 21.

He re-enlisted with The Royal Fusiliers and was serving as CSM with the 4th Battalion at the outbreak of World War I. This battalion was formed at Parkhurst IOW in 1914. It formed part of the 9th Brigade, 3rd Division and was one of the first to go to France – landing 13 August 1914. He saw action at Mons and in the Ypres Salient where he was again wounded. In January 1915 he was Mentioned in Dispatches and in June of the same year, by then a Warrant Officer (12391), he was awarded The Distinguished Conduct Medal (DCM). The citation was published in the London Gazette 30 June 1915 (29212). His DCM is recorded in the Regimental Honours Book but the circumstances are not mentioned in the war diaries. It is known that the battalion took severe losses during this time at Ypres.

A letter from his daughter Evelyn is held by The Imperial War Museum. Writing in 1974 she says:

> *In the words of a Brigadier General in 1917, father was a ... " good horseman and horsemaster. A very smart, clever Warrant Officer who can handle men and get the very best out of them..." he was also an excellent shot.*

He spent a period as an instructor at the School of Musketry in Hythe and was later commissioned. In September 1916 he won the Military Cross while serving with the 3rd Battalion The Royal Fusiliers. The award is not listed in the Regimental MC Book and again it has not been possible to trace the circumstances. He then transferred to the Army Service Corps. From 1918 he served with a British Military mission until he retired from the army with the rank of Captain to live at Hurstbourne House, Whaddon. He then worked as a NAAFI transport clerk and his daughter said he acted as a Special Constable in the 1926 "troubles".

At the outbreak of World War II William Foster was 61 years old and classed as a veteran. He joined the Alderbury Home Guard as a lieutenant shortly after its formation. While instructing a group of recruits on the techniques of throwing live grenades from a slit trench on Ashley Hill, a Mills bomb rebounded. Lt Foster immediately threw himself on the bomb, saving the lives of his comrades. He was posthumously awarded the George Cross, announced in the London Gazette on 27 September 1942. The citation read:

> *The KING has been graciously pleased to approve of the posthumous award of the GEORGE CROSS, in recognition of most conspicuous gallantry in carrying out hazardous work in a very brave manner. King George VI presented the decoration to his widow at Buckingham Palace.*

At a memorial service in St. Mary's Church on 12 January 1947, a tablet was dedicated to his memory by Lt Gen Sir John Crocker KBE CB CBE DSO MC, GOC Southern Command. Lieut Foster's widow and daughter in law were present alongside Major General Sir Harry Everett KCMG CB and the Vicar, Rev Basil Aston DSO. The stone tablet surmounts a replica of a George Cross surrounded by a laurel wreath. The tablet was provided by the Alderbury company of the Home Guard. There is a memorial bench to him situated on The Green bearing an inscribed plate.

His medal entitlement is GC, MC (GCR), DCM (GVR), Queen's South Africa Medal with clasps, King's South Africa Medal with clasps South Africa 1901 and South Africa 1902, 1914 Star with clasp "5 August-22 November 1914", British War Medal, Victory Medal with oak leaf (MID) and Defence Medal.

AEROPLANE CRASH IN ALDERBURY

One of the stories told in Alderbury is about an RAF Spitfire that crashed here in 1944 and is well remembered by the village children of the time. The following facts about that plane and its pilot have been discovered.

CECIL ERNEST BEARMAN
122343 Flight Lieutenant
131 Squadron, RAFVR
Died 25 August 1944. Aged 20.

HISTORY OF MD171 SPITFIRE HF VII

This plane had a Merlin 64 Engine. It was built in 1944, delivered to No 33 Maintenance Unit on 14 March and to 3501 Support Storage Unit the next day. On 17 June it was delivered to 131 Squadron. On 25 August 1944 it was listed as Flying Accident category F (written off), the day of Flt Lt Bearman's crash.

Cecil Ernest 'Pete' Bearman was born on 1 February 1917 in Saffron Walden, the second son of former Police Sergeant Henry and Harriett Bearman, of 16 Moulsham Drive, Chelmsford. He was educated at King Edward VI Grammar School in Chelmsford and then employed as a clerk with the Eastern National Omnibus Company. On 1 March 1937 'Pete' joined Essex County Constabulary (Police Constable 267, Serial Number 3573) and, after an initial period of training he saw service at Clacton. He returned to Headquarters in December 1937 to work on the motor patrols. After two years he was posted to Chelmsford and was awarded the Royal Humane Society's testimonial for his efforts with PC 635 Lacey to save a boy from drowning. He was subsequently posted to Romford in 1940 and remained there until enlistment.

On 24 May 1941 he became the first Essex policeman to join the RAF, and was the first to obtain his wings following training in Canada and the USA. He was killed on 25 August 1944, whilst leading a flight of 131 Squadron, he had been a flight commander for only two weeks. The Squadron had been equipped with the new high altitude Mark VII Spitfires in March that year and was involved in bomber escort duties. From May 1944 the squadron had been flying out of Culmhead (Church Stanton) five miles SE of Wellington in Somerset as part of D Day aircover.

He was flying Spitfire Mk VII MD171 and crashed at 9.50am when his aircraft dived into the ground out of cloud at military grid reference 635482, Alderbury Common. His body was recovered from the wreckage and taken initially to RAF Old Sarum. His funeral service was held at the London Road Congregational Church, Chelmsford on 1 September 1944 and he is buried in grave 5680 at Chelmsford Borough Cemetery.

In the late 1980s the crash site was extensively excavated in conjunction with the Longford Estate and some small pieces of fuselage and a glass dial were the only remaining fragments to be found.

CHAPTER 17

POST WAR 1947

Many other brave men and women from the area served in the forces during World War II and returned home safely. As a tribute to them the Parish Council ran a Welcome Home Fund for the ex-service men and women of Alderbury, Whaddon and Clarendon. Each person was given £2 and 133 Illuminated Addresses were framed and presented at a Welcome Home Party on 19 May 1947.

This photograph shows about 54 returnees.

Photograph courtesy of Salisbury Journal.

those who died will never be forgotten

those who survived will never forget

SOURCES

The main sources that were used in the research of both world wars are as follows: -

The Commonwealth War Graves Commission website

Contains information of an individual's battalion and regiment, date and place of burial and sometimes, name and address of next of kin. web-site: www.cwgc.org

Newspapers

The archives of The Salisbury Journal and The Salisbury Times are on microfilm at Salisbury Reference Library and contain notices of deaths, obituaries and other unclassified war information.

The National Archives at Kew

(TNA, formerly The Public Record Office)
www.nationalarchives.gov.uk

WWI medal index cards (WO372) and medal rolls (WO329)

These are also available for inspection online at TNA (for a small charge). A card contains details of regiment, number, date, the theatre of war abroad in which the soldier first served and medal entitlement. The index card is essential to access the medal rolls but these contain little additional information.

War Diaries

The original unit diaries (WO 95) are at TNA. They provide a fascinating look into a battalion's day-to-day life in a war zone. Although individual officers are often mentioned by name, it is unusual to find those of other ranks, unless cited for bravery. Typed copies can usually be accessed at regimental museums, by appointment. Those of the Royal Gloucester, Berkshire and Wiltshire Regiments (The Wardrobe, The Close, Salisbury) can be viewed on their website (www.thewardrobe.wardrobe.com). The curator, David Chilton, his staff and volunteers must be congratulated for their success with this project. Canadian Military Records and War Diaries for WWI and WWII are available online. (www.lac-bac.gc.ca/archivianet)

Service and Personnel Records of WWI

The War Office Depository in Arnside Street, London, where WWI service records were lodged after the war, was destroyed by a bomb in 1940 and most documents destroyed or badly damaged by fire and water. The remaining fragments are now at TNA and were recently made available on microfilm. They are better known as "the burnt documents" (WO363). Unfortunately, the records of men on the Alderbury War Memorials are not among them, nor among the Disability and Pension records (WO363).

Service records of the Royal Naval Division can be found in ADM 339 and most of the Royal Naval Volunteer Reserve in ADM 337 (also see below The Fleet Air Arm Museum).

Service and Personnel Records of WWII

These records are freely available to family members but the general public has only very limited access. Information can be obtained from: Ministry of Defence, Directorate of Personal Services (Army). We would like to thank them for their help and support in this project.

Other regimental records

The Guards Regiments keep their own records and information is available on request. The Fleet Air Arm Museum at Yeovilton, Somerset, has the attestation papers and service records of the men of the Royal Naval Division and the R N V R.
The National Archives of Australia and Canada are willing to send copies of attestation papers and service records of men who served and died in their forces. Fee applicable to cover photocopying and postage.

Soldiers Died in the Great War CD-Rom

A list was published in 1921 of the soldiers who died in the Great War with some details of enlistment and theatres of war. It can be accessed on the CD-Rom.

Army Roll of Honour

CD-Rom courtesy of The Royal Gloucestershire, Berkshire & Wiltshire Regiment (Salisbury) Museum. This is a comprehensive database of all who died in WWII.

1901 Census (England and Wales)

Residents who served in the 1914 – 18 war should be listed somewhere in this census.

1918 Electoral Rolls for Alderbury and Clarendon

Available at the Wiltshire Record Office, Trowbridge.

Regimental and Military Museums:

Fleet Air Arm Museum, Yeovilton, Somerset.
Royal Air Force Museum, Hendon, London NW9 5LL
RAF Air Historical Branch.
Royal Devonshire & Dorset Regimental Museum, Dorchester.
Royal Engineers, Brompton Barracks, Chatham, Kent
The Royal Hampshire Regimental Museum, Winchester.
Royal Corps of Signals Museum, Blandford Camp, Dorset.
The Royal Sussex Regiment Archives, County Hall, Chichester.
The Royal Sussex Regiment Museum, Eastbourne
The Royal Sussex Regiment Museum Trust, Rousillon Barracks, Chichester
The Queens Royal Surrey Regiment Museum, Clandon Park, Guildford
The Suffolk Regiment Archives. Colonel Taylor. 01603 400290
RRF Museum (Warwickshire) for The Royal Warwicks: David Baynham,
The Somerset Light Infantry (Prince Albert's), Taunton, Somerset.
Welsh Guards, Wellington Barracks, Birdcage Walk, London.
The Wiltshire Regiment (The Duke of Edinburgh's), Salisbury.
Scots Guards, Wellington Barracks, Birdcage Walk, London SW1E

Official Regimental Histories

These books give detailed assessment of the actions of their own battalions in specific theatres of war with explanatory maps and diagrams. They are essential for following the movements of individual companies or platoons. They also find casualty numbers. The books are sometimes available from public libraries through the inter-library request service or may be consulted at specific regimental museums by appointment.

Other organisations

Cemetery and Memorial Registers
Clarendon Park Estate Office
Dulwich College Archives
Dunkirk Memorial
Essex County Constabulary Records
Essex Police Museum, Chelmsford
Eton College Archives
Longford Estate Office
Portsmouth Police Archives.
Portsmouth Record Office
RAF Personnel Management Agency
Runnymede Memorial
St Dunstan's Archives
Victoria Cross & George Cross Association
West Sussex Record Office, Chichester

www.thewardrobe.org.uk The website of The Royal Gloucestershire, Berkshire and Wiltshire (Salisbury) Regiments. This provides a comprehensive study of regimental histories and an ongoing project to transcribe and publish, on-line, all the regimental War Diaries. WWI transcripts are currently on-line and WWII transcripts will be available once checked. The site has provided us with a large amount of valuable information.

www.gc-database.com The George Cross Database, a non-commercial web site, was founded in 2003 by the late Roger Hebblethwaite. It exists as an on-line tribute to all 401 recipients of the George Cross from 1940 to the present day. The comprehensive database gives each recipient their own page and is regularly updated as further information is received. We have worked with one of the authors of the site, Terry Hissey, to our mutual benefit.

www.hongkongwardiary.com and **www.lisbonmaru.com** The author of these sites, Tony Banham, is a Hong Kong Based researcher who was of great help in tracing the story of Norman Wathen and generously allowed us access to his research. He has thoroughly researched the history of the colony during WWII and is interested in hearing from anyone who may be connected to the *Lisbon Maru*.

www.essex.police.uk/memorial/roll.htm Essex Police Memorial Trust commemorates officers killed on duty, including those who were killed in both World Wars. Its biographical details proved informative and useful.

www.firstworldwar.com Comprehensive site in the form of an encyclopaedia.

www.regiments.org Details of regiments in worldwide armies. Detailed historical and present day British Army information.

MEDALS RELEVANT TO THIS BOOK

Medals in WWI Section

1914 Star awarded to members of the fighting forces who served in France and Belgium between 5 August 1914 and up to midnight of 23 November 1914 including the Royal Navy, the Royal Marines, the Royal Naval Division and the Royal Naval Volunteer Reserve. Civilian medical staff and nurses who accompanied them were eligible. It is sometimes incorrectly known as 'the Mons Star'.

The following three medals were popularly known as 'Pip', 'Squeak' and 'Wilfred'.

1914 – 1915 Star awarded to those who served in any theatre of war before 31 December 1915 and who were not entitled to the 1914 Star. Both medals could not be held at once. It rewarded those who had served before conscription started.

The British War Medal awarded to a member of a fighting force from anywhere in the British Empire who had left his native shore, whether or not he or she had served in a war zone.

The Victory Medal awarded to all who had entered a theatre of war. Every recipient who qualified for the Victory medal also qualified for the British War medal. Alderbury men who had enlisted with the Canadian and Australian forces, also qualified for these two medals.

The Memorial Plaque This was given to the next of kin of anyone in the services, or associated services, who died of any cause during the war at home or abroad, up to 1921. They were inscribed with the name of the casualty. For this reason they were sometimes called 'death plaques'. An illuminated scroll accompanied it.

Medals in WWII Section

George Cross the George Cross is the highest award for heroism by male and female persons in civilian and non-operational roles. The Royal Warrant was published in the London Gazette 31 January 1941.

Military Cross the award for "gallantry in the field" was instituted by Royal Warrant 31 December 1914 ......to be awarded to Officers whose distinguished and meritorious services have been brought to Our notice. It was a means of formally recognising the courage of junior officers, Captains and below, during wartime. It complemented the Military Medal awarded to non-commissioned officers.

Distinguished Conduct Medal (DCM) awarded for gallantry by non-commissioned officers from 1854, the D C M was regarded as second only to the Victoria Cross in prestige. It was superceded by the Military Medal in 1916.

1939 – 45 Star a Campaign Star awarded for service during WWII and considered as the "qualifying medal" in a series of eight awarded for service in various theatres of war. In the centre of each of the the six pointed stars is the Royal Cipher, surmounted by a crown. The whole is superimposed on a circle displaying the title of the Star.

The Atlantic Star awarded to commemorate the Battle of the Atlantic, it had a qualifying period of six months afloat.

Africa Star **(Eighth Army clasp)** awarded for service in North Africa between 10 June 1940 and 12 May 1943. One of the emblems awarded to this medal was the numeral eight for service in the 8th Army.

Pacific Star awarded for service in the Pacific theatre between 8 December 1941 and 2 September 1945. Service in Malaya between 8 December 1941 and 15 February 1942 was included.

Burma Star awarded for service in the Burma campaign between 11 December 1941 and 2 September 1945.

France & Germany Star awarded for any operation on land in France, Germany, Holland or Belgium between D Day and the German surrender, 6 June 1944 to 8 May 1945.

The Defence Medal awarded for three years of service in Gt Britain until 8 May 1945 or for 6months service under fire overseas.

War Medal 1939 – 45 awarded to all full time personnel of all the armed forces in both operational and non operational units.

India General Service Medal (37 – 39 clasp) awarded for service in India. The 1937-39 clasp was awarded to all personnel involved in operations on the North West Frontier.

Mentioned in Despatches: Oakleaves were awarded to anyone *"Mentioned in Despatches"*. These were worn on the medal ribbons.

WWII Medals had to be claimed by relatives.

SELECTED BIBLIOGRAPHY

WWI

Bruce Anthony. (2002) *The Last Crusade* – The Palestine Campaign in the First World War. John Murray, London.

Duckers Peter. (2003) *British Campaign Medals.* Shire.

Gilbert Martin. (1994) *First World War.* Weidenfeld and Nicholson, London.

Haythornthwaite Philip J. (1992) *World War One Source Book.* Arms and Armour Press.

Holding Norman. (1997) *World War 1 Army Ancestry.* Fed of Family History Soc. Ltd, Birmingham.

Holmes Richard. (1999) *The Western Front.* BBC. London.

Howard Michael. (2002) *The First World War.* Oxford University Press, Oxford.

Jerrold Douglas. (1921) *The Royal Naval Division.* Hutchinson & Co. London.

Jerrold Douglas. (1925) *The Hawke Battalion.* Ernest Benn, London.

Keegan John. *The First World War.* Hutchinson, London.

Middlebrook Martin (1983) *The Kaiser's Battle.* Penguin Books.

Moorehead Alan. (1973) Gallipoli. Andre Deutsch.

Page Christopher. (1999) *Command in the Royal Naval Division: a military biography of Brigadier General A M Asquith DSO.* Spelmount. Staplehurst. Tonbridge, Kent.

Spencer William. (2001) *Army Service Records of the First World War.* PRO. Kew.

Swinnerton Iain. (2001) *Identifying your World War I Soldier from Badges and Photographs.* FFHS(Publications)Ltd.

Retallack John. (1981) *The Welsh Guards.* Frederick Warne. London.

Simkins Peter. (2002) *Essential Histories: The First World War 3: The Western Front 1917-18.* Osprey. Oxford.

Westwell Ian. (2000) *World War 1 – Day by Day.* Grange.

Whithorn David P. (2003) *Bringing Uncle Albert Home – A Soldier's Tale.* Sutton. Stroud Glos.

WWII

Alderbury & Whaddon LHRG. (2000) *Alderbury & Whaddon: A Millennium Mosaic of People, Places and Progress.*

Action Station 5 – Military Airfields of the South West. Patrick Steven Ltd, Sparkford Yeovil. (courtesy of RAF Museum, Hendon).

Ball Robert WD. (1996) *Collectors Guide to British Army Campaign Medals.* Antique Trader Books (R355 1342).

Banham Tony. (2003) *Not the Slightest Chance – The Defence of Hong Kong 1941.* Hong Kong University Press.

Brown David, Shores Christopher, Macksey Kenneth. (1976). *The Guinness History of Air Warfare.* Purnell Book Services Ltd.

Buckman Richard. (2001) *The Royal Sussex Regiment Military Honours and Awards 1864-1920.* J&KH Publishers, Hailsham.

Buckman Richard. (2001) *The Royal Sussex Regiment Military Honours and Awards 1921-66.* J&KH Publishers, Hailsham.

Chorley WR. (1996) *RAF Bomber Command Losses 1943.* Midland Counties Publications, Leicester.

Eggenberger David. (1967) *A Dictionary of Battles.* Allen & Unwin.

Erskine David. (1956) *The Scots Guards 1919-1955.* William Clowes & Son.

Fighter Squadrons of the RAF and their Aircraft. Crecy Books. (courtesy of RAF Museum, Hendon).

Forbes Patrick. *6th Guards Tank Brigade, Guardsmen in Tanks.* Sampson Low Marshall & Co.

Johnson RB Maj. (1997) *The Queens in the Middle East and North Africa 1939 – 1943.* The Queens Royal Surrey Regiment.

Kinvig Clifford. (1992) *River Kwai Railway.* Brassey UK.

Nicholson Col W.N. CMG DSO. *The History of The Suffolk Regiment 1928-46.* East Anglian Magazine, Ipswich.

Pakenham Walsh H.P. Maj-Gen. (1958) *History of the Corps of Royal Engineers Vol VIII.* Institution of Royal Engineers, Chatham.

Paul Christopher Air Commodore. (1989) *Sing High, History of 90 Squadron.* 90Squadron Assoc.

The Queens Royal Surrey Regiment. (1997) *The Queens in the Middle East and North Africa 1939-43.*

Macdonald Patrick. *The Suffolk Regiment, 1st Battalion in Belgium and the Netherlands 1944.*

Wheal Elizabeth-Anne & Pope Stephen. (1997) *Macmillan Dictionary of The Second World War.* Macmillan.

INDEX

Albery, Charles Ernest, 41-2
Albery family, 41
Albery, Maisie, 41
Alderbury Bowls Club, 101
Alderbury Common, 119
Alderbury Farm (Fort's Farm), 44
Alderbury Hill House Lodge, Clarendon, 70
Alderbury School, 42, 60, 65, 101
Alderbury Village Band, 42
Angel, Albert, 71-3
Angel, John & Nelly, 72
Aquitania, 45
Ashley Hill, Clarendon, 118
Ashley Hill House, Clarendon, 94
Asquith, Arthur, 45
Australian Division, 32-4

Bailey, Lena, 68-9
Bailey, Robert, 71
Barber, Charles, 71
Bartlam, Frederick, 71
Bearman, Cecil Ernest, 119
Bearman, Henry & Harriet, 119
Beavan, Charles Hazel, 54
Beavan family, 54
Belmont Cottages, Clarendon, 64-5
Belmont House, Clarendon, 64
Belstone, Abraham, 71
Bishop Wordsworth's School, Salisbury, 72, 101
Bowden, Leonard, 71
Brewer, Frederick, 71
Brewer, Jesse, 71
Brewer, Walter, 71
Bundy, Arthur Cecil, 20, 26-7
Bundy, Edward & Evelyn, 20, 26
Bundy, Ernest Noyce, 20-2, 26-7
Bundy family, 20, 26, 28, 63
Bundy, Robert & Ellen, 28, 63
Bundy, Robert Henry, 28, 62-4
Bundy, Samuel, 72
Bundy, Samuel & Charlotte, 49
Bundy, Thomas Pearman, 24, 28-9, 63
Bundy, Walter Joshua, 46, 49-50
Bundy, William, 20, 26, 71
Bundy, Winnifred Anne, 28
Burt, Archibald Frank, 60

Canadian Infantry Regt. 49-50
Canadian Mounted Rifles, 20-2, 26-7, 46-9
Carse, Alan, 71
Carter, Frederick William, 80-1
Carter, George & Florence, 81
Cherry Tree Cottage, Old Road, Alderbury, 36
Chowringhee House Lodge, Clarendon, 69-70
Christie-Miller, Michael Vandeleur, 104-5, 109
Christie-Miller, Sydney Richardson 104

Clarendon, Alderbury Hill House Lodge, 70
Clarendon, Ashley Hill, 118
Clarendon, Ashley Hill House, 94
Clarendon, Belmont Cottages, 64-5
Clarendon, Belmont House, 64
Clarendon, Chowringhee House, 70
Clarendon, Four Cottages, 116
Clarendon, Kennel Farm, 65
Clarendon Home Guard, 104, 117-9
Clarendon Park, Clarendon, 104
Clarendon Road, Alderbury, 57, 81, 84, 87
Coldstream Guards Regt, 104-5, 108-9
Cook, Ellen, 42
Coole, Albert, 71
Court House, Alderbury, 49
Cox, George, 71
Cox, Harry, 71, 73
Cox, Henry, 72
Cox, John, 72
Crook, Ernest, 72

Dean, Charles, 71
Dean, William, 72
Devanha, 32
Devonshire Regt, 24, 38-9
Dicks, Ernest, 71
Dicks, George, 72
Dorsetshire Regt, 42-3, 66-7, 70, 91
Dowding, Josiah, 71
Dowty, Albert, 71
Dowty, Edwin, 71
Dowty, Edwin G, 71
Dowty, Frederick, 71
Dummer, Hannah, 41

Earney, Edward Thomas, 69-70
Earney, Victor, 70-1
Earney, William James & Phoebe, 70
East Grimstead School, 116
Elliott, Will, 68
England, Harry, 71
England, Ronald, 71
England, Victor, 61, 71
Eyres, Victor, 61, 71

Ferry Cottage, Shute End, 18,
Firs Road, Alderbury, 101
Fisherton Anger, Salisbury
Forge (The), Old Road, Alderbury, 32
Fort's Farm, Alderbury, 44
Foster, George, 117
Foster, William, 117-8
Four Cottages, Clarendon, 116
Fry, Gilbert, 71
Fry, Percy, 71

Gables (The), Southampton Road, Alderbury, 108
Gambling, Frederick, 71
Geelong, 32

General Service Corps, 116
Godolphin School, Salisbury, 42
Gray, Howard, 71
Gray, Ralph, 71
Gray, Stanley, 71
Green Howards Regt, 90
Grenadier Guards Regt
Grout, Edward George, 80, 86-7
Grout, George & Sarah, 87
Gulliver, Charles, 71
Gumbleton family, 111
Gumbleton, Stanley Kenneth, 104, 110-2
Gumbleton, Walter & Mary, 111

Hallett, Albert, 71
Hampshire Regt, 28, 30, 63-4
Harper, Francis George, 50
Harris, Frank, 71
Hatcher, Arnold William, 90-2
Hatcher, Arthur & Laura, 57
Hatcher, Claude, 71
Hatcher, Edward, 24-6, 57, 71
Hatcher, Edward & Annie, 25, 30
Hatcher, Ernest Henry,
Hatcher family, 42, 57
Hatcher, Frederick Charles, 57-9
Hatcher, John Phillip, 25, 28, 30
Hatcher, Maurice, 71
Hatcher, Percy, 57, 71
Hatcher, Samuel & Alethea, 42-3
Hatcher, Sidney, 71
Hatcher, Sidney & Edith Agnes, 91
Hatcher, William, 25, 71
Hawtin, Victor, 72
Hazel, Gwen, 18
Hazel, Sydney, 18-9,
Hazel, Thomas, 18, 71
Hazel, William & Alice Ann, 18
Hickman, Jesse, 71
Hickman's shop, High Street, Alderbury, 42
HMS Agincourt, 18
HMS Collingwood, 111
HMS Forester, 110-3
HMS Hampshire, 18-9, 22
HMS Impregnable, 18
HMS Prince of Wales, 86
HMS Ramilies, 111
HMS Repulse, 86
HMS St Vincent, 111
HMS Venus, 18
HMS Victory, 18
Home Guard, 104, 117-9
Howe, Alfred, 34, 36-7
Howe family, 36
Howe, Jack, 36
Hutchings, James, 71
Hyman, William, 72

Ingram, George & Anna, 44-5
Ingram, Harry, 71

Ingram, William, 34, 44-6

Jervis, Thomas, 72

Kemp, Charles, 71
Kennel Farm, Clarendon, 65
Kerly, Florence, 65
Kerly, Harold, 65
Kerly, Maurice Adolphus, 64
Kerly, Walter & Ellen, 64
Kidd, John Walter Cameron, 98-100
King Edward VI Grammar School,
    Chelmsford, 119
King's Royal Rifle Corps, 95
Kirkby family, 115
Kirkby, Samuel Alexander Holwell, 80,
    114-5
Kitchener, Field Marshall Earl, 19, 22

Ladies Cottages, Whaddon, 54, 91
Lakonia, 93
Lancastria, 80
Lander, Clarence, 71
Lever, Bertram, 71
Lisbon Maru, 84-5
Littleton, Junction Road, Alderbury
Lock, Harry, 71
London Regiment, 55
Longford Castle, 114-5
Longford Estate, 42, 49, 99, 116, 119

Machine Gun Corps, 28-9, 71
Maidment, Algernon, 71
Maidment, Cyril, 71
Maidment, Felton, 71
Maidment, Hedley, 71
Malmesbury Secondary School, 99
Mason, William, 71
Matrons College Farm, 38
McLeod, Roderick Campbell, 90, 94-7
McLeod, Sir Murdoch Campbell, 94
Meadows (The), Whaddon, 116
Middlesex Regt, 23-4
Mitchell, Arthur, 116
Mitchell, Sidney Charles, 116
Moody, Wilfred, 71
Mouland, Bertram, 32
Mouland, Edgar, 31-3
Mouland family, 32
Mouland, John & Emma, 32
Mouland, Ralph, 71
Mouland, Reginald, 32, 71
Mouland, Wilfred, 26-7, 32, 46-8
Mount Pleasant, Folly Lane, Alderbury,
    66
Musselwhite, Harry, 68-9
Musselwhite, James & Emma, 68
MV Johann van Oldenbarnvelt, 91, 93

Newell, William, 71
Newman, Cecil, 71
Northard, E., 102
Northeast, Albert, 55-6
Northeast, Charles George & Agnes,
    66-7
Northeast, Edward & Jane, 55

Northeast family, 55
Northeast, Frederick, 71
Northeast, James, 55, 71
Northeast, Leslie Leonard, 66-7
Northeast, Thomas, 71
Northeast, Victor, 66, 72

Oaklands, Clarendon Road, Alderbury,
    72
Occomore's Bakery, 101
Old Road, Alderbury, 59
Osmond family, 70
Osmond, Percival, 71
Oxford & Buckinghamshire Light
    Infantry, 65

Parfitt, Ethelbert, 71
Parry, Beryl, 43
Pearce, Edith, 87
Pearman, Edith Eleanor, 23
Pearman family, 24
Pearman, Thomas Charles, 23-4
Pearman, Thomas Holloway &
    Rosalind Alice, 24
Pennsylvania, Alderbury, 87
Pines Cottage, Whaddon, 25
Pines (The), Whaddon, 111
Prewett family, 37
Prewett, Frederick, 37, 71
Prewett, Harry, 34, 37-8
Prewett, Henry James & Louisa, 37
Prewett, Mary, 36
Prewett, William, 37, 71

Queen's Royal Regiment, 90-2

Reading Room Cottage, Old Road,
    Alderbury, 73
Richardson, Stanley, 71
Richardson, William, 71
Rolls, Alfred, 39, 72
Rolls family, 39
Rolls, George & Elizabeth 39, 61
Rolls, Hedley Robert, 39, 61
Rolls, Reynold George, 39, 61-2
Rolls, William, 39, 71
Rose Cottage, Silver Street, Alderbury,
    99
Royal Air Force, 98-102
Royal Army Service Corps, 87-8
Royal Army Veterinary Corps, 73
Royal Corps of Signals, 84-5
Royal Engineers, 54, 56, 80-1
Royal Field Artillery, 39
Royal Fusiliers Regt, 72
Royal Naval Division, 44-6, 57-9
Royal Regiment of Artillery, 116-7
Royal Scots Regt, 66-7
Royal Sussex Regt, 114
Royal Warwickshire Regt, 55-6
Royal Welsh Fusiliers Regt, 73
Rumbold's Lane, Whaddon, 55
Rumbold, Thomas, 71, 73
Russell, Harry, 72
Russell, Reginald, 71
Russell, William, 71

Scots Guards Regt, 90, 94
Sheppard, Charles, 72
Shorter, Alfred, 72
Shorter, Percy, 72
Shute End, 18
Silver Street (37), Alderbury, 20
Sims, Harry & Emma, 59
Sims, Herbert, 72
Sims, Henry John, 59-60
Snook family, 101
Snook, Jack William, 98, 100-2
Snook, William & Ada, 101
Somerset Light Infantry, 51, 59, 61
Somme, Junction Road, Alderbury, 24
Southampton Road (25-26),
    Alderbury, 37
Southampton Road, Whaddon, 30
Spring Cottage, West Grimstead, 116
SS Lapland, 47
SS Missanabie, 49
Suffolk Regt, 107-8

Tanglin, Firs Road, Alderbury, 41
Tanner, Walter, 72
Thomas, Frank, 72
Totterdown Cottage, Folly Lane,
    Alderbury, 73
Tozer, Hugh Henry, 38
Tozer, Thomas William & Annie Meaby,
    38
Trusler, Bessie, 65
Tucker, Charles, 72
Turner, Charles Edward, 116-7
Turner family, 116
Turner, William, 116

USS Grouper, 84-5

Vicarage Lane, Alderbury, 39, 61
Vincent, Charles, 72
Vincent, William, 72

Walden Cottage, West Grimstead, 68
Warwickshire Regt
Wathen family, 84
Wathen, Tom & Emily, 84
Wathen, Walter Norman, 84-5
Welsh Guards Regt, 24-6
Whaddon Brickworks, 116
Whaddon Cottage, Whaddon, 45
Whitcher, Lionel, 72
White, Walter, 72
Williams, Elizabeth Mary, 25
Willis, Frederick, 72
Willis, Henry, 72
Willis, William, 72
Wiltshire Regt, 25, 28, 32, 34, 36-7, 39,
    41-2, 51-2, 60-1, 68-9
Winchester College, 95
Witt, Cyril, 109
Witt family, 109
Witt, William Day & Winnifred
    Blanche, 109
Woodrow family, 107-8
Woodrow, Jack Attwood, 107-8
Woodrow, William Archibald, 107-8